THE LITTLE BOOK OF
TENNIS

Written by **John Thynne**

THE LITTLE BOOK OF
TENNIS

This edition first published in the UK in 2009
By Green Umbrella Publishing

© Green Umbrella Publishing 2009

www.gupublishing.co.uk

Publishers Jules Gammond and Vanessa Gardner

Printed and bound in Poland

ISBN: 978-1-906635-65-7

Contents

Agassi

▶ With his long hair and good looks, Agassi was a fans' favourite.

Lightning reactions, powerful groundstrokes and one of the best service returns in history helped Andre Agassi to win all four Grand Slam tournaments during his career – a feat only managed by five male players to date.

A favourite with the fans, in his early years he was renowned for his long hair and colourful dress sense. A tough fighter on court (he is the son of an Olympic boxer), the Las Vegan wore his emotions on his sleeve and is probably best remembered for his moving 6-7, 6-4, 6-4, 1-6, 6-4 triumph over Goran Ivanisevic in the 1992 Wimbledon final.

Despite the fact he had already played in three Grand Slam finals, few believed the American had what it took to win on grass, but victories over Boris Becker in the quarters and John McEnroe in the last four showed he could go all the way. After an intense struggle on the second Sunday, Ivanisevic's famous service finally deserted him. Agassi seized his first match point opportunity and slumped to the ground, burying his face in the Wimbledon turf. Although he claimed another seven Major titles, an Olympic gold medal and a spell as world number one, he was unable to repeat his feat at SW19.

Married to seven-time ladies' Wimbledon champion Steffi Graf, Agassi has two children – Jaden Gil and Jaz Elle.

All England

Although it hosts the Wimbledon Championships at the end of June/beginning of July every year, few people realise the All England Tennis and Croquet Club is also a private members' establishment.

Numerous permanent grounds staff and maintenance workers look after the extensive 42-acre site, which boasts 19 main and 22 practice grass courts, five red shale courts, three clay and five indoor courts.

There are in the region of 400 full members of the All England, and each

has access to the club's facilities – other than Centre Court and No 1, which are saved for Wimbledon – all year round.

As well as Wimbledon itself, the club is occasionally used for Davis Cup ties and in 2012 will be the venue for the Olympic tennis tournament – 90 years after it first moved to its present site in Church Road, SW19. Within the grounds, the Wimbledon Lawn Tennis Museum houses everything from the famous championship trophies to fascinating examples of tennis attire through the ages.

▲ The new roof on Centre Court under construction, September 2008.

◄ Crowds watch the men's singles final, 2008.

Ashe

In tennis terms, Arthur Robert Ashe Jr will be remembered for his shock defeat of Jimmy Connors in the 1975 Wimbledon final. But the American's legacy runs far deeper than that.

Born in Virginia in the racially segregated South, Ashe had obstacles placed in his way from the outset. Forced to fight for the right to play in "whites-only" tournaments, he quickly established his reputation as a gifted athlete.

Ashe retired after an unexpected heart attack in 1979 and later learned he had contracted Aids, probably from a tainted blood transfusion during surgery in 1983. Already a tireless charity campaigner, he launched the Arthur Ashe Foundation for the Defeat of Aids in 1992 but tragically died the following year.

During his playing career Ashe won 33 singles titles, including the 1968 US Open and 1970 Australian Open. At the age of 31 and seeded sixth, he came up against firm favourite and world number one Jimmy Connors in the 1975 final at the All England. Using a well thought out strategy, Ashe employed subtle spins, changes of pace and wide, swinging serves to his opponent's double-handed backhand, frustrating Connors and ultimately winning 6-1, 6-1, 5-7, 6-4. The first black male player to win a Grand Slam title, he remains the only black men's Wimbledon singles champion.

Australian Open

The first of the four Grand Slam tennis tournaments held each year, the Australian Open is played at Melbourne Park in Victoria, south-east Australia.

The championship was first held in 1905 on the lawns of the Warehouseman's Cricket Club and it remained a grass court event until 1987, after which the tournament moved to its present home. Now a hard court competition, it is currently played on a surface called Plexicushion.

The competition has had various guises during its history. Originally named the "Australasian Men's Championships", it was actually held in New Zealand in 1906 and 1912, before changing its name to the "Australian Championships" in 1927. In 1969, the tournament was opened up to amateurs and took on the familiar "Open" tag we know today.

Much has changed since those early

▼ The "True Blue" Plexicushion surface at the Australian Open.

▼ Jo-Wilfried Tsonga plays a forehand return at the Australian Open.

days when Rodney Heath defeated Dr Arthur Curtis in front of a crowd of 5,000 in the very first final. For a start, women are very much involved – the first ladies' championship was held in 1922, Margaret Molesworth overcoming Esna Boyd in the final.

Nowadays more than half a million tennis fans surge through the gates during the course of Open fortnight each year and in excess of 17,000 watched the 2008 final showdown between Novak Djokovic and Jo-Wilfried Tsonga.

There are 24 courts at Melbourne Park, including five show courts. Two of these – the Rod Laver Arena and the Hisense Arena – have retractable roofs which means play can continue in extreme weather conditions.

Australian legend Roy Emerson holds the record for the highest number of singles titles with six victories between 1961 and 1967, while Andre Agassi has set the "open" era benchmark with four wins, one more than both Sweden's Mats Wilander and Swiss maestro Roger Federer. Another famous Aussie, Margaret Court, boasts the women's record with 11 championships to her name.

Wilander was the youngest ever men's singles champion when he defeated Ivan Lendl in the 1983 final aged 19 years 111 days. Meanwhile, Ken Rosewall was the oldest ever champion at 37 years two months when he beat fellow Aussie Mal Anderson 7-6, 6-3, 7-5 in 1972. The youngest women's singles champion in history was Martina Hingis, who defeated Mary Pierce aged 16 years three months in 1997. In the women's game, Thelma Long took the 1954 title four months short of her 36th birthday.

Sadly, the Australian crowds have been without a "home-grown" winner since Christine O'Neil in 1978 – Lleyton Hewitt was the last native star to reach a singles final (against Marat Safin in 2005).

Ball

So reads Appendix 1a in the International Tennis Federation's rules but the exact regulations governing balls run to several hundred words.

There are three main types of ball approved for competition today, designed for play on slow, medium and fast paced courts. All must fall within set "rebound" parameters – they must bounce between 53in and 58in when dropped from a height of 100in onto a "smooth, rigid and horizontal surface". Furthermore there are strict size limits and rules governing the amount a ball "deforms" – there are even guidelines for high altitude tennis.

The modern pressurised tennis ball consists of two rubber "half-shells" which are moulded together to produce a core. This is covered in a wool or nylon cloth that is usually yellow – Wimbledon used traditional white balls until 1986.

▼ Yellow Wilson balls are the preferred option at the Australian Open.

Becker

"Boom Boom" Boris Becker exploded into the public consciousness in 1985 when, aged just 17 years seven months, he claimed the biggest prize of them all. Becker's unexpected victory over America's Kevin Curren in the Wimbledon final heralded a new era in "power" tennis and the German remains the youngest ever champion at the All England.

While nobody had expected Becker to win the championship, the seeds of his momentous victory were sewn a year earlier when he reached the third round at SW19 before being forced to retire through injury.

Becker then reached the quarter-finals of the Australian Open before claiming his first ATP Tour title – at Queen's Club – on June 17 1985. His decisive 6-2, 6-3 defeat of Johan Kriek in the final on the grass courts of West Kensington was the shape of things to come.

At the All England, the young German survived a scare against Joakim Nystrom in the second round and staved off two match points against Tim Mayotte in the last 16. Four-set wins over Henri Leconte and Anders Jarryd put the boy from Leimen in the final against Curren, 10 years his senior.

Curren himself was in fine form having beaten defending champion John McEnroe and two-time Wimbledon winner Jimmy Connors on his way to the final, but the American had

no answer to Becker's aggressive groundstrokes, accurate, powerful serving and athletic net game. The youngster triumphed 6-3, 6-7, 7-6, 6-4 to become the first German and first unseeded player to win Wimbledon.

Becker went on to beat Ivan Lendl in the 1986 final but came up against Sweden's Stefan Edberg in the last two in '88. This was the beginning of one of tennis' famous rivalries, the Swede taking the title that year, the German triumphing in '89 and Edberg once again winning in '90. Becker would reach the final one more time but was forced to give way to another German with a mighty serve – Michael Stich.

Becker claimed three more Grand Slam titles during his career, taking the Australian Opens of 1991 and '96 and the US Open in '89. He also added two Davis Cup victories and an Olympic gold medal to his CV, but the German will forever be associated with Wimbledon. He finally bade goodbye to the Centre Court after losing in the fourth round in 1999. "It was a great love affair," Becker said afterwards. "It was like nowhere else in the world. The place was always very special to me. It made who I am today."

▲ Boris Becker in action at Wimbledon.

Blake

A world top-10 ranking, good looks and more than £3.5 million banked in prize money to date – you'd think James Riley Blake had it all. But success hasn't come easy to the American, who has overcome a series of setbacks to become the superstar he is today.

Diagnosed with scoliosis (curvature of the spine) when he was a teenager, for five years Blake was forced to spend 18 hours a day in a back brace. But the talented youngster with the fast footwork and huge forehand didn't let it hold him back and by his second season at Harvard was the number one player on the collegiate circuit.

He turned pro in 1999 and quickly rose up the rankings until in 2004 he had an accident that threatened to put an end to his tennis career. During practice he stumbled while running at full speed and collided with the net post, breaking his neck. His father tragically died of cancer the same year and Blake was later diagnosed with shingles which temporarily paralysed the left side of his face and gave him sight problems.

Undeterred, this athlete-cum-model fought back and has become a permanent fixture in the top 20 since February 2006. Although he has never progressed beyond the quarter-finals of a Grand Slam singles, his victory over Roger Federer in the last eight at the Beijing Olympics shows the New Yorker's potential. He has bagged 10 singles titles to date and helped his country to victory in the 2007 Davis Cup.

Borg

With 11 Grand Slam tournament wins to his name, Bjorn Borg sits fourth in the all-time list, but it is for his five consecutive Wimbledon victories that the steely Swede is best remembered.

Supremely fit, mentally untouchable and boasting rock-solid, heavily top-spun groundstrokes, the Ice Man made Centre Court his own between 1976 and 1980.

His most impressive triumphs were perhaps his first and last. In '76 the Swede outclassed all opposition to win the championship without dropping a set – a feat that has not been equalled since. His opponent in the final that year was the wonderfully talented Ilie Nastase, but the Romanian had no answer to the flaxen-haired double-hander, succumbing 6-4, 6-2, 9-7.

Four years later Borg was to face John McEnroe on Centre Court in what many believe was the greatest Wimbledon final of all time. The Swede had two championship points at 5-4 in the fourth set but his 21-year-old opponent – playing in his first Wimbledon final – clung on to force a

▲ Borg prepares to play a low backhand shot.

a top-spin backhand which the Swede could only half-volley into the net.

A lesser player would have been demoralised by such an outcome but Borg fought on to the bitter end, eventually taking his eighth match point with a cross-court backhand against the McEnroe serve.

Borg would face McEnroe again in the final of 1981, but although he won the first set he later said he lacked "that sparkling feeling". McEnroe then won two tie-breaks and took the fourth set 6-4 to end Borg's 41-match unbeaten streak at the All England. The Swede went on to reach the US Open final that year but his Wimbledon defeat was the beginning of the end. Borg played just one tournament in 1982 and retired the following year, aged just 26.

Of course, there was more to Borg than Wimbledon. The Swede won a record six Roland Garros titles and, until Rafael Nadal in 2008, was the last player to do the Wimbledon-French Open double in the same season. Over a period of four years between 1977 and '81 he traded the world number one ranking with Jimmy Connors and his great rival McEnroe, the Swede holding the top spot for a total of 109 weeks.

tie-break that defined both men's careers.

The pair traded blows for an incredible 22 minutes in that tie-break, each holding a series of set or, in Borg's case, championship points. Ultimately it was McEnroe who triumphed, driving

Budge

John Donald Budge was the first man to claim a singles Grand Slam – that is he won Wimbledon and the Australian, French and US Opens in the same calendar year – and is believed by many to have been the greatest player of them all.

Having won Wimbledon and the US Open in 1937, Budge had been tempted to turn professional but decided to remain in the unpaid ranks for what would turn out to be an incredible final year.

A straight sets Australian Open final victory over John Bromwich was complemented by a 6-3, 6-2, 6-4 triumph over Czechoslovakia's Roderich Menzel at Roland Garros. Big-serving Budge would drop just four games in the 1938 Wimbledon final against home favourite Bunny Austin, and he completed the perfect set at Forest Hills, defeating fellow Davis Cupper Gene Mako 6-3, 6-8, 6-2, 6-1 in the US Open final. The Grand Slam was his and the feat would not be equalled for another 24 years.

Budge is also remembered for one

▲ An athletic Don Budge in action.

of the most thrilling Davis Cup matches of all time. In the deciding game of the Cup's inter-zone final against Germany in 1937, Budge recovered from two sets and 4-1 down to defeat Baron Gottfried von Cramm, taking the US into the Challenge round against Britain. The States went on to beat the home side at Wimbledon, Budge winning each of his three matches.

Burn-Out

▶ Shoulder injuries forced Andrea Jaeger out of the game at a young age.

The tennis world is a uniquely pressurised one and the demands of the sport have claimed plenty of victims at an early age. Alongside the major success stories there are plenty of players who have shown great potential, yet suddenly slipped down the rankings or quit altogether. Often these players have done "too much, too young", a phenomenon sometimes referred to as "burn-out".

Many believe America's Andrea Jaeger experienced a classic case of burn-out. Winning US collegiate tournaments at the age of 13, she was claiming pro titles at 14 and by 15 had reached the semi-finals of the US Open. She is best remembered for reaching the Wimbledon final in 1983. Although she had only just turned 18, Jaeger stormed through the draw at SW19 without losing a set, defeating Billie Jean King 6-1, 6-1 in the semi-final. But in the final against Martina Navratilova, Jaeger suffered a 6-0, 6-3 defeat in under an hour. Sadly we had seen the best of the young American – a shoulder injury saw her retire by 1987. Nowadays

she devotes her life to the Episcopal Church and has raised millions for sick or disadvantaged children through her Little Star Foundation.

Cash

A natural serve-volleyer, Wimbledon provided the perfect arena for Patrick Hart Cash. Already a former junior champion, he is best remembered for his emotional victory over Ivan Lendl in the men's singles final of 1987.

Wearing his trademark black-and-white checked bandana, Cash took the first two sets 7-6, 6-2 and at 6-5 in the third found himself serving for the championship. Sealing the deal with a cross-court forehand volley, the Australian raised his arms in a two-fisted show of exultation before climbing through the crowd to embrace friends and family in the players' box.

Cash was never able to repeat that performance although he did reach the final of the Australian Open for a second time in 1988, heartbreakingly losing in his home event to Sweden's Mats Wilander, 6-3, 6-7, 3-6, 6-1, 8-6.

▲ Pat Cash on his way to his only Wimbledon triumph.

The Australian, who reached a career-high world ranking of four, helped his country to Davis Cup victory twice. In 1983, aged 17, he became the youngest player ever to represent the winning side in a final when Australia overcame Sweden. And he proved the Swedes' nemesis once again in 1986, thrilling the home crowd by coming back from two sets down to defeat Mikael Pernfors in the deciding rubber.

A regular on the senior tennis scene and a respected commentator, Cash's other love is music – he is guitarist in his own band, The Wild Colonial Boys.

Connolly

The majority of Maureen Connolly's tennis career was sandwiched into four short years but in that time 5ft 4in

"Little Mo" staked her claim as one of the best female players of all time.

By the beginning of 1953, the bubbly 18-year-old from San Diego with the fast footwork and powerful strokes already had three Major titles to her name but even she could not have foreseen what was in store for her. Over the next few months she claimed the US, French, Wimbledon and Australian Championships, thus becoming the first ever woman to record a Grand Slam.

In '54 she joined a select group of players to do the "treble" at Roland Garros, winning the singles, doubles and mixed doubles, before going on to successfully defend her title at the All England. But disaster struck soon afterwards when she injured her right leg in a riding accident and was forced to retire from the game in her prime.

The year after her accident she married Norman Brinker, a former member of the US Olympic equestrian team and they were to have two children. She continued to teach the game but in 1966 was diagnosed with cancer and tragically died three years later, aged just 34.

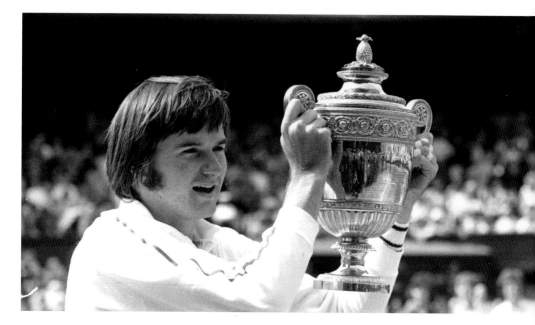

Connors

An often controversial but always entertaining figure, Jimmy Connors was one of a kind. Defying old age he continued to compete at the highest level until the age of 40, amassing 109 singles titles, including five US Opens, two Wimbledons and an Australian

Open along the way.

The boy from Belleville, Illinois, was introduced to the game by his teaching professional mother, Gloria, and showed potential from a very young age. He became renowned for his street-fighting style and unorthodox strokes, which included a fierce two-handed backhand. Supremely fit, he would run for every ball and his never-say-die attitude made

▲ Jimmy Connors after his win over Ken Rosewall at Wimbledon in 1974.

◀ Maureen Connolly holding the Wimbledon trophy.

▲ Jimmy Connors pulling a cheeky face.

him a fearsome opponent.

This refusal to give up was never better exemplified than in the fourth round of the 1987 Wimbledon Championships against the hapless Mikael Pernfors. The Swede played superbly for two and a half sets to lead the number seven seed 6-1, 6-1, 4-1, but Connors would not throw in the towel. In a supreme gesture of fist-pumping defiance, the American recovered to take the third set. A shell-shocked Pernfors was unable to respond to the rejuvenated Connors, the American going on to take the next two sets 6-4, 6-2.

Connors' true love affair, however, was with the US Open. Not only is he the sole player to have won the tournament on three different surfaces – on grass in 1974, clay in '76 and on hard courts in 78, '82 and '83 – but in 1991 he pulled off one of the most extraordinary achievements in modern tennis. A wildcard entrant, he dragged himself through the draw to the semi-finals, and although he ultimately went down in straight sets to number four seed Jim Courier, Connors had recorded an incredible string of results, including a dramatic five-set victory over Aaron Krickstein on his 39th birthday.

James Scott Connors topped the world rankings for an incredible 160 consecutive weeks in the mid-1970s, a record that would remain unbroken for 30 years until a certain Roger Federer finally bettered it in 2007, and continued to trade the number one spot with great rivals Bjorn Borg, John McEnroe and Ivan Lendl until 1983. In addition to his Grand Slam singles victories, he claimed two doubles Majors – Wimbledon in 1973 and the US Open in 1975 – with Ilie Nastase. He was inducted into the International Tennis Hall of Fame in 1998.

Court

The second of three women to achieve the calendar Grand Slam, Margaret Court's career is all about records.

With 24 Big Four singles titles to her name she is the most successful player in terms of number of individual Major titles won. Court, who played under her maiden name, Smith, until 1967, also won 19 doubles events and 19 mixed, taking her Grand Slam total to an incredible 62 – another record.

Her "big" year was 1970. Having defeated compatriot Kerry Melville Reid in two sets at the Australian Open and Germany's Helga Niessen 6-2, 6-4 in the French Open final, she met Billie Jean King on the second Saturday at the All England. The third leg of the Slam produced what many believe to be the greatest women's Wimbledon final of all. Following a riveting, two-and-a-half hour struggle, the Australian finally triumphed 14-12, 11-9. The 46-game battle set a record for the number of games played in a women's final at Wimbledon.

The last piece in the jigsaw was to be found at Forest Hills and the US Open where Court overcame a stutter in the second set to defeat home favourite Rosie Casals and emulate "Little Mo" Connolly's four-out-of-four feat of 1953.

▼ Margaret Court preparing to serve.

Davis Cup

D

▼ The very successful Davis Cup team of the Four Musketeers.

The Davis Cup is tennis' foremost international men's team competition, and for more than a century it has produced a heady mix of

drama, emotion and sporting prowess to rival any of the Grand Slams. Only 12 nations have claimed the famous silver trophy, the United States holding the record for most victories with 32.

Today more than 120 countries take part in the event but the competition had very humble beginnings. The brainchild of one Dwight Davis, a student at America's Harvard University, the first Davis Cup was a challenge match between the United States and Great Britain. Davis himself played in the inaugural tie as the home side triumphed 3-0 at Longwood Cricket Club in Boston.

In 1903 the British claimed the first of their nine trophies and by 1905 the Belgians, French and Australasians (their team represented New Zealand and Australia) were on board. In 1927 the French began to take charge and, led by the famous Four Musketeers – Jean Borotra, Jacques Brugnon, Henri Cochet and Rene Lacoste – they would take six consecutive Cups.

Until 1972, the reigning champions progressed directly to the final each year, where they awaited a "challenger" that had come through the main draw. Up until this point countries such as

Australia – led by Harry Hopman for more than 20 years and containing luminaries such as Frank Sedgman, Lew Hoad, Ken Rosewall, Rod Laver and Roy Emerson – and the United States had dominated the event, but now they too would be forced to compete in each round of the Cup every year. From this point on the competition opened up to a degree, the likes of South Africa (1974), Sweden ('75), and Italy ('76) claiming memorable victories.

The Cup is a statistician's dream, with all manner of extraordinary records achieved over the past 108 years. The player with the most appearances in the competition is Italy's Nikki Pietrangeli – he took part in 66 ties and played 164 matches – while the longest ever individual game lasted an incredible six hours and 22 minutes, John McEnroe of the United States eventually defeating Sweden's Mats Wilander 9-7, 6-2, 15-17, 3-6, 8-6 in 1982.

Tie-breaks have obviously shortened the length of matches but the event has undergone other significant changes over the years. Today the competition is split into a 16-strong "World Group" and three continental zones, each of which contains a further four groups.

Relegation and promotion between the groups takes place annually but only teams playing in the World Group can actually claim the Cup each year.

▲ The Davis Cup trophy.

▼ Spain's Fernando Verdasco serves to Argentina's Jose Acasuso during the Davis Cup final, 2008.

Djokovic

At just 21 years of age, Novak Djokovic is considered by many to be the future of top-level tennis. Rising into the top 20 in 2006 via a quarter-final appearance at the French Open, 2007 was the 6ft 2in Serb's big breakthrough year.

He reached the fourth round in Melbourne before losing to Roger Federer, and then the semi-finals at both Roland Garros and Wimbledon in quick succession, going down on each occasion to Rafael Nadal.

In September that year, and by now firmly cemented as world number three, he made his first Grand Slam final appearance at Flushing Meadows, once again coming up against Federer. Although the Serb would lose in straight sets, two tie-breaks showed he had what it took to challenge the then world number one.

Djokovic broke his Grand Slam duck in the very next Major, beating Federer in the semi-finals and then Jo-Wilfried Tsonga – the conqueror of Nadal – at the 2008 Australian Open. Two more Grand Slam semi-finals would follow that year, while Djokovic also added a bronze Olympic medal to his glowing CV.

Boasting solid groundstrokes on both sides, a powerful serve and the ability to perform at the net when he needs to, it's difficult to see a weakness in his game. A popular player with the fans, he is renowned for his amusing impersonations of other tennis stars.

Dod

Charlotte "Lottie" Dod was known as "The Little Wonder". And although that moniker referred to her tennis abilities, it is even more apt when applied to her life as a whole. Not only did the girl from Bebington in Cheshire win five Wimbledon singles titles but she triumphed in the 1904 British Ladies Amateur golf championship, claimed an archery silver medal at the 1908 Olympics and represented her country at hockey.

When Dod won her first Wimbledon in 1887 she was just 15 years 285 days old and she remains the youngest ever singles champion (Martina Hingis of Switzerland was three days younger when she won the ladies' doubles with the Czech Republic's Helena Sukova in 1996). Each of Dod's finals was played against Blanche Bingley (Blanche Hillyard from 1888), and it was only in her final appearance at Wimbledon in 1893 that she struggled against her London rival. Dod recovered after losing the first set to ultimately triumph 6-8, 6-1, 6-4.

Courtesy of victories in 1891 and

◄ Lottie Dod, ladies' Wimbledon singles champion on five occasions.

'92, Dod had become the first woman to win three Wimbledon singles titles in a row. Of course, this was the era of the "Challenge round" – the reigning champion was not required to play the early stages of the tournament, and instead waited for a contender to emerge from the main draw. Nevertheless, her record stood until France's Suzanne Lenglen pulled off a string of five successive victories between 1919 and '23.

Doubles

While the majority of the limelight is reserved for the Federers, Nadals, Williams and Sharapovas of this world, a number of supremely talented players ply their trade on the international doubles circuit.

Good doubles players need to have reliable serves, solid overheads and lightning-quick reactions as many rallies involve sharp volleying exchanges at the net. Doubles specialists such as American brothers Bob and Mike Bryan possess these qualities in abundance and have earned millions of dollars on the ATP circuit without ever having made a huge impact on the singles scene. In women's tennis, neither Cara Black nor Liezel Huber have troubled the higher echelons of the individual game – but put them together and you have one of the most potent doubles teams in history.

Other highly successful doubles combos from the past include Aussie pair Mark Woodforde and Todd Woodbridge (the "Woodies"), who dominated in the 1990s, and Americans Ken Flach and Robert

Seguso, who shone in the mid-1980s. Although accomplished singles players in their own right, all of these players enjoyed more success as doubles exponents.

There was a time though, when doubles was popular among the greatest singles players on the planet. Take John McEnroe – not only did the gifted American claim seven Grand Slam singles titles, he teamed up with compatriot Peter Fleming to win four Wimbledon and three US Open doubles titles. Later in his career he won a further US Open title with Woodforde and then teamed up with top-10 singles star Michael Stich to win Wimbledon in 1992 at the age of 33.

Other big-name singles players of the 1960s and '70s who teamed up to win doubles Grand Slam titles included Jimmy Connors and Ilie Nastase, Ken Rosewall and Lew Hoad, Roy Emerson and Rod Laver, and John Newcombe and Tony Roche.

In the women's game the likes of Martina Navratilova, Billie Jean King, Margaret Court and Maria Bueno have succeeded at both singles and doubles and in recent years the likes of the

Williams sisters at Wimbledon have given the format a publicity boost.

Mixed doubles has been played by the very top stars too. Navratilova has won four mixed titles at Wimbledon, most recently with India's Leander Paes in 2003, while Ilie Nastase of Romania and America's Rosie Casals won two Wimbledons together in the early 1970s.

▲ Leander Paes and Cara Black after winning the mixed doubles title at the 2008 US Open.

◀ The victorious pairing of Michael Stich and John McEnroe at Wimbledon.

Down Under

It has always been a strong tennis–playing nation but during the 1960s Australia's men ruled the world. Between 1960 and '69 Australians claimed 32 of the 40 Grand Slam tournaments available, courtesy of the finest batch of players to ever grace the courts.

An incredible 23 of those victories fell to just two men, Roy Stanley Emerson and Rodney George Laver, two of the most celebrated Australian sportsmen in history – but more about them elsewhere in this book. Neale Fraser, Fred Stolle, Tony Roche, John Newcombe, Bill Bowrey and Ken Rosewall complete the list of Grand Slam champions from the 1960s, the likes of moustachioed Newcombe and the elegant Rosewall going on to even greater glories in the '70s.

With such an incredible line-up of champions it's not difficult to see why Australia claimed seven Davis Cups during the '60s under the leadership of the notoriously tough Harry Hopman.

The groundwork for this era of Aussie dominance had in fact been done by the likes of Frank Sedgman, Lew Hoad, and Ashley Cooper during the '50s. Hoad came within a whisker of the Grand Slam in 1956. Having won the Australian, French and Wimbledon Championships, he fell at the final hurdle, losing the climax of the US Open to Rosewall.

But it wasn't just in the men's arena that the Aussies were dominating. Margaret Court had her own Grand Slam franchise in the '60s, winning 16 titles during that period, and she was ably assisted by Lesley Turner-Bowrey (she married Bill Bowrey in 1968) who claimed the French Open Championships of 1963 and '65. Between 1964 and '74, the Australians won seven Fed Cups (the female equivalent of the Davis Cup), courtesy of Court, Turner-Bowrey, Judy Tegart, Kerry Melville, Judy Dalton, Karen Krantzcke, Evonne Goolagong, Lesley Hunt, Patricia Coleman, Janet Young and Dianne Fromholtz.

Goolagong, of course, found individual fame as one of the best players of the 1970s. The Aboriginal superstar, who became Evonne Goolagong Cawley following her marriage to British tennis player Roger Cawley, won four Australian Opens, one French and two Wimbledon titles during a glittering career and was briefly ranked world number one.

Since the 1970s, the Antipodeans have lost their grip on the game somewhat although the likes of Pat Cash, Pat Rafter and Lleyton Hewitt have claimed the occasional Grand Slam title. Things have gone quieter still in the women's game – Goolagong was the last Australian female to win a Major – the 1980 Wimbledon crown.

Edberg

▶ Stefan Edberg reaches for a backhand.

An elegant, even-tempered player, Stefan Edberg was at the peak of his powers during the late 1980s and early '90s. Becoming world number one for the first time in 1990, the tall, blond Swede won six Grand Slam titles, only the French Open eluding him.

A natural serve-volleyer, he was most at home on the grass courts of Wimbledon, where he took two titles, defeating Boris Becker in the finals of 1988 and 1990. His main weapons were a backhand drive that was at once supremely powerful and impossibly graceful, and an incisive serve. In fact, many players feared the Swede's second service more than his first, due to its awkward, high-kicking bounce.

Edberg's first Major victory came at the 1985 Australian Open – then played on grass at Kooyong Lawn Tennis Club – where he defeated Mats Wilander in straight sets. He would triumph once again in Melbourne two years later in the last Australian Open to be played on grass, but this time he needed five sets to defeat home favourite Pat Cash.

Edberg proved he wasn't a one-surface-wonder in Grand Slam terms by winning the 1991 and '92 US Open but could never quite come to terms with the clay of Roland Garros, his best result a runner-up spot to Michael Chang in 1989.

Emerson

"Emmo" belonged to Australia's – and for that matter tennis' – golden era. The athletic six-footer from Blackbutt, Queensland, won 12 Grand Slam singles titles and sits third behind Pete Sampras and Roger Federer on the all-time list.

Roy Stanley Emerson was renowned as one of the fittest players in the game and for his wicked forehand. During a stellar career which peaked as the amateur era drew to a close, Emerson bagged six Australian Opens, two titles at Stade Roland Garros, two Wimbledons and two US Open Championships.

One of a select group to have achieved a "career Grand Slam" (only five players have won each of the four Majors at some point in their careers – Emerson, Fred Perry, Don Budge, Rod Laver, and Andre Agassi) Emerson's achievements were not confined to the individual game. He won a further 16 Big Four doubles titles and, incredibly, was on the winning side in eight Davis Cups, where he formed irresistible partnerships with Neale Fraser and Fred Stolle as well as winning numerous vital singles rubbers.

His final doubles Grand Slam title came at Wimbledon in 1971, when, aged 34, he teamed up with Laver to defeat Arthur Ashe and Dennis Ralston 4-6, 9-7, 6-8, 6-4, 6-4 in an epic match.

▼ Roy Emerson with the Wimbledon trophy in 1965.

Evert

► Chris Evert after winning at Wimbledon in 1974.

▼ Chris Evert stretches for a ball.

During a 16-year period that ended in 1988, America's Chris Evert played in 34 Grand Slam singles finals, winning 18 – a record that would no doubt have been even more impressive had it not been for a certain Czech nemesis by the name of Martina Navratilova.

A relentless baseline hitter, Evert had the better of Navratilova on the clay courts of the Stade Roland Garros, beating her rival in the final on three occasions and losing just once. In fact, boasting seven titles in total, Evert still holds the record for the most singles victories in Paris.

However, there is little doubt Navratilova had the edge at Wimbledon and the unfortunate Evert lost out five times in the final to her serve-volleying rival. That is not to say Evert could not play on grass – she won at SW19 in 1974, '76 (beating Navratilova in the semis) and '81 and defeated Navratilova in the 1982 Australian Open final when it was held on the surface.

Throw in another Australian win in '84 and six victories in her home tournament, the US Open, and it is easy to see why Evert was inducted into the International Tennis Hall of Fame in 1995.

Through her Chris Evert Charities, the American star has helped to raise millions of dollars for needy children and their families in Florida.

Fans

Type "Rafael Nadal" into an internet search engine and you will find more than six million sites related to the Spanish star. That is a small indicator of the interest in the game and you only have to see the pictures from Flushing Meadows, Melbourne Park or Roland Garros to recognise the passion tennis enthusiasts globally have for the game.

More than 10 million people in Britain tuned in to watch Andy Murray's fourth-round victory over Richard Gasquet at Wimbledon during 2008 – including more than half of Scotland's potential audience! Scenes of "Murraymania" are now commonplace at the All England with fans arriving in ever-more colourful garb, their faces painted with Union Jacks or Scottish saltires.

And such is the passion among

British fans at SW19, that a grassy mound in Aorangi Park, from which spectators can watch a giant screen displaying key matches, has been christened "Henman Hill" after perennial British semi-finalist Tim Henman.

Wimbledon is so popular that fans have to enter a public ballot for show court tickets each year. Scenes of early-morning queues around the grounds are now legendary as anxious supporters from all over the world wait for the chance to buy one of the 500 tickets available daily (except for the last four days) for Centre, No 1 and No 2 courts.

▲ Fans flock to Henman Hill to watch their idol in action.

Fashion

▶ Tennis attire at the turn of the 20th century.

▼ Anne White wearing an unusual one piece outfit.

We've come a long way from the white trousers and full-length dresses of tennis' yesteryear – in fact we've seen some pretty unusual outfits over the last few decades, some of which the players might rather forget!

Who can forget the skin-tight, all white bodysuit worn by America's Anne White at Wimbledon in 1985 or Dominik Hrbaty's shirt with big holes in the back that he sported at the US Open of 2005?

In fact clothing controversy has been around for decades. One of the earlier players to break the mould was Suzanne Lenglen in the 1920s. The Frenchwoman dared to bare her arms and wear dresses that finished around the calves as well as brightly coloured cardigans and

headwear. Meanwhile Britain's Bunny Austin introduced shorts to the men's game in 1932.

In the end it's all about making your mark. For example, Andre Agassi once made a sartorial name for himself with an array of outfits that featured bandanas, pirate headscarves and luminous cycling shorts worn under denim, while Roger Federer prefers the refined, cardigan and blazer look.

One modern player who knows a thing or two about fashion is Venus Williams. The American Wimbledon champion recently graduated from fashion school and launched her own clothing line.

Fed Cup

The Fed Cup is the equivalent of the Davis Cup for female tennis players and has been running for more than 40 years.

American player Hazel Hotchkiss Wightman (of Wightman Cup fame) came up with the concept of an international women's team competition in 1919 but it was not until Nell Hopman and Mary Hardwick Hare took up the baton that the Cup eventually became a reality in 1963.

Known as the "Federation Cup" until 1994, the United States is by far the most successful nation historically and during the '60s, '70s and '80s

was able to draw on the likes of Billie Jean King, Rosie Casals, Chris Evert, Tracy Austin and Martina Navratilova (who was also in Czechoslovakia's winning team in 1975!). In fact between 1976 and '82 the US went on a seven-year winning streak that remains a Fed Cup record.

In recent years a new generation of Russian players has begun to dominate. Featuring the likes of Svetlana Kuznetsova, Anastasia Myskina, Elena Dementieva, Dinara Safina and Vera Zvonareva, the Eastern European side claimed four out of five Cups between 2004 and 2008, and with such a wealth of talent in the world's top 20, the trend looks likely to continue.

▲ The winning Russian team in 2008.

◀ Serving at the Fed Cup.

Federer

Few players deserve the title "legend" but, aged just 27, Roger Federer has already secured an exalted place in tennis history. In an age of power hitting, the Swiss star still manages to look graceful on the court, at times defying belief with his speed and anticipation.

Immediately recognisable for his flowing groundstrokes and exaggerated follow-throughs, Federer appears to have it all, boasting a variety of service options and solid volleys. Recording an unprecedented 237 consecutive weeks as the number one player in the ATP rankings and boasting 13 Grand Slam singles titles, he is now engaged in a fascinating rivalry with Spanish star, Rafael Nadal.

In 2007 Federer equalled Bjorn Borg's feat of five Wimbledon victories in a row and came agonisingly close to a sixth in what many believe was the best ever final at the All England in 2008. Having lost the first two sets, Federer staged a comeback but, in the gathering gloom, finally had to concede defeat in the fifth after 288 minutes of enthralling tennis.

In 2008 Federer claimed a fifth US Open Championship to add to his three Australian titles, as he drew within one of Pete Sampras' record number of Grand Slam singles victories. But he will not be content until he wins the one big tournament that has so far eluded him. Although an accomplished clay court player, to date Federer has been unable to win at Stade Roland Garros, and that is largely down to his Spanish nemesis – Nadal defeated him in three consecutive finals between 2006 and 2008.

Despite his relative youth, Federer has played in three Olympic Games but has been unsuccessful in the singles event, his best run ending in semi-final defeat in Sydney. He made up for this to some extent at Beijing in 2008, teaming up with Stanislas Wawrinka in the men's doubles. An unexpected victory over America's Bryan brothers in the last four was followed by a four-set triumph over

Sweden's Simon Aspelin and Thomas Johansson, as the Swiss pair doubled their country's final gold medal tally.

By the end of 2008, Federer had amassed more than $43 million in career earnings, surpassing Pete Sampras' record. Now one of the richest sportsmen on the planet, Federer has become a household name and one of the greatest – if not the greatest – players in the history of the game.

▼ Roger Federer makes a backhand return.

F

Ferrer

▶ David Ferrer
serves to his
opponent.

▼ David
Ferrer plays a
double-handed
backhand.

David Ferrer may not be as famous as compatriot Rafael Nadal, but the 27-year-old Spaniard has quietly confirmed himself as one of the best players in the world over the past couple of years.

A determined campaigner, Ferrer is capable of frustrating more powerful players with his tireless running and relentless consistency.

But despite being a permanent fixture in the world's top 20 since August 2005 and with a career-high ranking of four, Ferrer has yet to fulfil his potential in the biggest tournaments. Although he has claimed seven singles titles across the world, the long-haired Spaniard has only once reached the semi-final of a Grand Slam event – the 2007 US Open – where he was defeated by Novak Djokovic in straight sets.

Ferrer is one of a group of sublimely talented Spanish players currently on the world stage and in 2008 he helped his country to Davis Cup victory, recording a remarkable 7-6, 2-6, 1-6, 6-4, 8-6 victory over America's Andy Roddick in the semi-finals.

French Open

Played on red clay courts – the slowest of the Grand Slam surfaces – the French Open is held at Stade Roland Garros in Paris at the end of May each year. It is the second Major on the international tennis calendar and traditionally concludes two weeks before the start of Wimbledon.

Between 1891 and 1924, the French men's singles championship was a purely domestic affair – it was not until '25 that the competition became an international event. The tournament moved to its present-day venue near Port d'Auteuil three years later when a purpose-built tennis facility was created, principally to host France's defence of the Davis Cup. The stadium was named after one of Stade Francais' most famous former members – French aviator Roland Garros, the first man to fly a plane over the Mediterranean. The first international men's singles champion was Rene Lacoste, who on that occasion defeated fellow French "Musketeer" Jean Borotra. Meanwhile, the French heroine Suzanne Lenglen overcame Britain's

▲ The red clay court of Philippe Chatrier at Roland Garros.

Conseil International en
Immobilier d'Entreprises

▲ Mats Wilander and Yannick Noah walking out at the French Open, 1983.

greatest matches in the history of tennis.

The names of Rod Laver, Ilie Nastase, Ivan Lendl, Mats Wilander and Jim Courier are all etched on the famous Coupe des Mousquetaires, but the man who really made Roland Garros his home was Bjorn Borg. Champion in 1974, '75, '78, '79, '80 and '81, the Swede still holds the record for the most French wins.

Fascinatingly, though, a number of big names are conspicuous by their absence. Jimmy Connors, John McEnroe, Boris Becker, Stefan Edberg and Pete Sampras were unable to convert their magical talent into victory in Paris. This is largely due to the fact their games were not ideally suited to the slower clay surface.

In the women's game, as previously mentioned, Chris Evert reigns supreme with her seven singles titles.

In 2000 the home crowd were able to celebrate the first victory by a Frenchwoman since the open era began when Mary Pierce defeated Conchita Martinez 6-2, 7-5 in the final. Only Yannick Noah has triumphed for France in the open era men's singles, his 1983 win going down in the nation's tennis folklore.

Kitty Godfree in the women's final.

In 1968, Roland Garros, as the tournament was by then known, was opened up to professionals as the truly "open" era began, and since that date Paris has been witness to some of the

Gasquet

Boasting a fine all-court game, France's Richard Gasquet is arguably one of the most gifted players on the circuit. A former world junior number one, he has often played with the weight of a nation's expectations on his shoulders, although the current proliferation of French talent in the world's top 20 should help ease that burden.

Where the Grand Slams are concerned the Frenchman is most at home at Wimbledon, his finest hour to date coming in 2007 when he came back from two sets down in the quarter-finals to defeat Andy Roddick 8-6 in the fifth.

The following year he came up against Andy Murray in what British fans will remember as one of the most exciting games in the championships' history. The Frenchman strolled through the first two sets but Murray staged a spirited comeback, and, egged on by a partisan crowd, the Scot finally triumphed 5-7, 3-6, 7-6, 6-2, 6-4. Despite this setback, one senses there is more to come from Gasquet at SW19.

Although there is huge pressure on Gasquet to perform, commentators seem to forget he is still only 22.

He broke into the world's top 10 for the first time in July 2007 and has remained in the top 30 ever since.

Gonzales

Today "success" in tennis is often measured by number of Grand Slam singles titles won and at first look, Richard Alonso Gonzales, with two US Open victories to his credit, seems far from remarkable. But during the late 1950s "Pancho" was arguably the best on the planet.

It has to be remembered that Wimbledon as well as the Australian, French and US Opens were not open to professional players until the late 1960s and following his American wins in 1948 and '49 Gonzales joined the paid ranks, touring with the great Jack Kramer in a series of exhibition matches. By the mid-1950s, the Los Angeles–born Gonzales was unstoppable. A perpetual US Pro champion and winner of the London Pro Championships at Wembley in 1950, '51, '52 and '56, Gonzales was a match for anyone. In 1966, by now aged 38, he defeated Ken Rosewall and Rod Laver to win the BBC2 Tournament at Wembley and in 1968 reached the semi-finals of the French Championships and quarters at the US Open.

Somewhat unfairly, Gonzales is remembered by most for his five-hour, 22-24, 1-6, 16-14, 6-3, 11-9 victory over Charlie Pasarell in the first round at Wimbledon in 1969. But that is to do a disservice to the great man, who with his unstoppable serve and deft touch, was, at the peak of his powers perhaps the finest ever to play the game.

THE LITTLE BOOK OF TENNIS

Navratilova in three sets at Wimbledon gave the 19-year-old German the chance to emulate Maureen Connolly and Margaret Court and claim the holy grail of tennis – the Grand Slam. In the US Open at Flushing Meadows, Graf rocketed through the draw, losing just 13 games on her way to the final where she came up against Argentinean fifth seed Gabriela Sabatini. Following a stutter in the second set Graf finally

◄ Steffi Graf with the Wimbledon trophy in 1996.

▼ Steffi Graf plays a backhand return.

Graf

Graceful, athletic and powerful, Steffi Graf reigned for a total of 377 weeks as women's number one during the 1980s and '90s but her finest achievement came in 1988 when she claimed the calendar year Grand Slam.

That year a straight sets defeat of America's Chris Evert in the Australian Open was followed by a 6-0, 6-0 demolition of the unfortunate Natalia Zvereva in the final at Roland Garros. Victory over perennial rival Martina

1993, only a three-set loss to Monica Seles in the Melbourne final denying her another perfect year.

Never one to court the limelight, Graf let her tennis do most of the talking. The winner of 22 Grand Slam singles titles during her career, her greatest weapons were supreme athleticism and the strongest forehand the women's game has ever seen. So good was the right-hander's footwork that she would often run around her backhand to pound her opponent with sledgehammer forehands. Graf is sometimes unfairly criticised for having a "weak" backhand but in fact her sliced shot across the body was a potent weapon that kept rivals pinned to the baseline. In later years the German added a top-spin shot to her armoury but still tended to prefer the sliced version.

Unlike many great players, Graf retired at the top of her game in August 1999. Still ranked number three in the world, earlier that year she had claimed her sixth French Open title, defeating Martina Hingis in a three-set thriller, and reached her ninth Wimbledon final.

Graf married fellow tennis great, Andre Agassi, in 2001.

triumphed 6-3, 3-6, 6-1 to forever seal her place in tennis' pantheon of greats.

In 1988 the German also won the gold medal in the Seoul Olympic Games, urging commentators to dub her achievements a "Golden Grand Slam", a feat that has yet to be equalled in the men's or women's games. In fact Graf came close to another Big Four in

Grand Slam

The term "Grand Slam" is principally used to refer to the achievement of winning all four of tennis' Major tournaments – the US Open, French Open, Wimbledon and Australian Open – in the same calendar year. It is seen as the ultimate accomplishment in tennis due to the variety of court surfaces involved and the fact that all the best players in the world compete at each of these events.

Only three women – Maureen Connolly, Margaret Court and Steffi Graf – have achieved this extraordinary feat in the women's game, while Don Budge and Rod Laver are the only men to have "won the Grand Slam".

Over the years variations on the theme have been recorded. Someone who has claimed each of the Big Four tournaments "at some point during their career" is said to have won a "Career Grand Slam", while Steffi Graf became the only player to win a "Golden Slam" in 1988 when she took the singles title at the Olympics as well as each of the four Majors. Several players – notably Martina Navratilova – have achieved "Non Calendar Year Grand Slams", that is they became the holders of all four Major crowns simultaneously but did not win them all in the same year.

It is also possible to win a men's doubles, women's doubles, or mixed doubles "Grand Slam" – for example Frank Sedgman and Ken McGregor of Australia won each of the four men's doubles titles during 1951.

▲▲ Rod Laver won a Grand Slam.

▲ Grand Slam winners Frank Sedgman and Ken McGregor.

Henman

On November 20 1995, 21-year-old Timothy Henry Henman of Oxford broke into the world's top 100 for the first time – and who could have foreseen what an impact he would have on British tennis?

By 1996 he had reached the quarter-finals at Wimbledon and two years later he went one stage further, giving home fans something to really shout about for the first time since Roger Taylor reached the last four in 1973.

In fact Henman's career is unavoidably defined by the championships at the All England. A natural, elegant serve and volleyer, "Tiger" Tim's game was ideally suited to grass, and Henman – whose grandfather and great grandmother both played at Wimbledon – reached the quarters at SW19 eight times in a nine-year period, progressing to the semis four times.

His finest hour came in 2001 when, after dispatching (15th seed!) Roger Federer, he came up against Croatian wildcard Goran Ivanisevic in the semi-finals. After losing the first set the Englishman had the typically partisan crowd – and millions of supporters at home – on the edges of their seats as

only did he win 11 main tour singles titles, he reached a career high of number four in the world and in 2004 reached the semi-finals at both the French and US Opens, proving he could cope with any surface. He also won 40 of his 54 Davis Cup matches, fittingly retiring from the game in 2007 after helping Great Britain back into the elite World Group with victory over Croatia.

In 2004 Henman made a trip to Buckingham Palace to receive the OBE from the Queen for his services to the game and he now has a successful career as a commentator at Wimbledon.

◀ Tim Henman serves during Wimbledon fortnight, 2007.

◀◀ Henman plays a forehand.

▼ Fans on "Henman Hill" watching him in action.

he proceeded to take a tie-break and then the third set 6-0. It appeared the momentum was with Henman but rain interrupted play and Ivanisevic came back stronger, finally triumphing 7-5, 6-7, 0-6, 7-6, 6-3.

After the match the Croat said: "This is destiny. God wanted me to win this game – he sent the rains." Ivanisevic then went on to win perhaps the most emotional Wimbledon final ever – but more on that elsewhere in this book.

Of course, Henman achieved some superb results outside of Britain. Not

Hewitt

◀ Lleyton Hewitt celebrates his victory over David Nalbandian in 2002.

▼ Lleyton Hewitt runs the baseline to return a shot from Pete Sampras.

The youngest ever player to achieve a world number one ranking (aged 20 years, eight months), Adelaide-born Lleyton Hewitt has bagged two Grand Slam singles titles.

In 2001, the fiery baseliner defeated Pete Sampras 7-6, 6-1, 6-1 to claim the US Open and the following year he demolished David Nalbandian 6-1, 6-3, 6-2 in the final at Wimbledon, having dropped just two sets throughout the tournament.

During an impressive career, the South Australian has racked up 26 main

tour singles titles, banked more than $17 million in prize money and been on two Davis Cup winning sides. But despite his prodigious talent and long spell as the number one player on the planet, many believe Hewitt should have won more of the Big Ones. To date he has not progressed beyond the quarter-finals at the French Open and has been unable to end his nation's win drought at the Australian Open, despite a valiant effort in 2005 when he reached the final against Russia's Marat Safin.

Known for his work ethic and determination, Hewitt had injury problems in 2008 and slipped down the world rankings – but most believe it would be a mistake to write off one of nature's born fighters just yet.

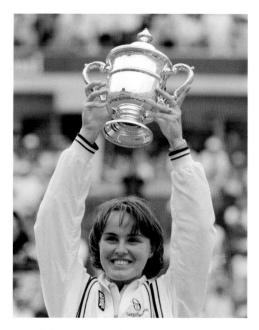
Hingis

Before she had even reached her 20th birthday, Martina Hingis had won five Grand Slam titles, and she remains the youngest player ever to be rated number one in the world (at 16 years, six months and one day).

Born in Slovakia in 1980, Hingis moved to Switzerland at the age of eight and went on to represent her adopted country in 14 Fed Cup ties, including an appearance in the 1998 final against Spain.

Renowned for her court craft and accuracy, Hingis used guile and intelligence as well as wonderful touch to outwit her opponents, but in later years the relentless hitting of the new generation of "power players" became harder to combat.

The Swiss player was at the height of her powers in 1997 when she claimed the Australian Open, Wimbledon and US Open titles, only Croatia's Iva Majoli denying her a clean sweep in the final at Roland Garros. But in 2003, aged just 22, Hingis retired from the professional game after persistent ankle problems. In 2006 she showed remarkable determination, returning to the tour and fighting back to number six in the world. But her comeback was short-lived as she quit the game for good the following year.

One of the few players to have reached number one in both singles and doubles simultaneously, Hingis also won nine Grand Slam pairs titles, most memorably with Jana Novotna.

▲ Martina Hingis with the US Open trophy after victory over Venus Williams in 1997.

History

▲ A game of real tennis.

▶ Tennis rackets of yesteryear.

As a form of amusement, humans have been hitting balls to each other for hundreds – if not thousands – of years. There is evidence that European monks played a form of tennis using leather gloves to propel the ball and "jeu de paume" ("the game of the palm") was popular in France from as early as the 14th century. At some point rackets were introduced to the equation and "real tennis" – played indoors on a court that featured sloping roofs and indentations off which shots could be played – became a popular pastime.

Real tennis is still played today although it is not anywhere near as popular as its modern descendant, lawn tennis, which came about towards the end of the 19th century when Major Walter Clopton Wingfield introduced a version of the game that could be played outside on grass. By 1877 England's Spencer Gore had won the very first Wimbledon Championships and played his part in the evolution of the sport played by Nadal, Federer, Sharapova and the Williams sisters today.

Technology, attire and style of play may have changed over the past 130 years or so but the principles of the game remain the same.

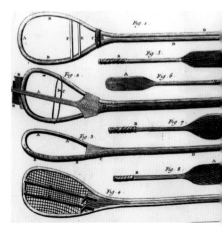

If...

"*If you can meet with triumph and disaster and treat those two impostors just the same*". These are the words written in bold capitals above the players' entrance to Centre Court at Wimbledon.

The lines, which form just a small part of Rudyard Kipling's famous poem, *If*, perfectly sum up the ethos of sportsmanship that has historically run through the game. In tennis terms they seem to be telling the players that both victory and defeat are transient; neither matter in the grand scheme of things — what's most important is the game itself and how you behave, regardless of the result.

A board featuring the inscription was first installed at the All England in 1923. Presented to the club by Lord Curzon, the original can still be seen at the Wimbledon Lawn Tennis Museum within the grounds.

In 2008 the BBC broadcast a reading of the entire poem by men's finalists, Rafael Nadal and Roger Federer, before the pair produced one of the most thrilling matches ever played at Wimbledon.

▲ Wimbledon Lawn Tennis Museum.

▼ *If*, the poem above the entrance to Centre Court at Wimbledon.

In!

Knowing whether a ball has landed "in" or "out" is critical in a game of tennis and disputes over line calls are common at all levels.

At Wimbledon, 10 line judges and a chair umpire officiate on each match on Centre, No 1 and No 2 courts and, considering some of the top players are serving at well over 130mph and that ball speeds can reach 50m per second, you can see why they are needed.

But humans are prone to error – which is where state of the art technology comes in. The Cyclops system uses infrared beams to determine whether serves are in or out, and spectators will now be familiar with Hawk-Eye, which utilises cameras and sophisticated computer software to create a graphical representation of a ball's flight path.

Implemented at the Australian and US Opens as well as Wimbledon, players can request a Hawk-Eye video replay of a particular point if they doubt the decision of an official.

In 2008 the main tennis governing bodies agreed to adopt a unified system at tournaments using Hawk-Eye, under which players were permitted to make three unsuccessful "challenges" per set (a further failed challenge is permitted in a tie-break).

Ivanisevic

Wimbledon 2001. Goran Ivanisevic, the beaten finalist in 1992, '94 and '98 had fallen to number 125 in the world rankings and needed a wildcard entry to the championships.

But his big serve had not deserted him and he bludgeoned his way through the draw, defeating Andy Roddick, Marat Safin, Greg Rusedski and Tim Henman along the way to reach the last two for a fourth and final time. His opponent there was Australia's Patrick Rafter, runner-up the previous year, a consistently nice guy with a point to prove.

The tournament had run over to a third Monday and a raucous Wimbledon crowd was joined by millions of tennis enthusiasts surreptitiously turning on television sets at work as the most fascinating duel unravelled.

Inevitably the match went to a fifth set and the Croatian was just two points from defeat at 6-7. But he dug deep, held serve and broke Rafter to set up the most emotional final game of all.

Teary-eyed, the man from Split twice double-faulted on championship point. Another match point slipped through his fingers and the 29-year-old's agony was palpable. But after three hours of mesmerising tennis, Rafter finally submitted and Ivanisevic fell to the ground, his lifetime's ambition complete.

◄ Goran Ivanisevic with the Wimbledon trophy.

▼ Goran Ivanisevic in tears after winning at Wimbledon.

Ivanovic

▶ Ana Ivanovic with the French Open trophy, 2008.

▼ Ana Ivanovic stretching to hit a backhand.

Serbia's Ana Ivanovic broke into the general public's consciousness in 2007 when she reached her first Grand Slam final at Roland Garros. Having comfortably defeated Russian second seed Maria Sharapova in the last four, Ivanovic took on reigning champion Justine Henin, and the then 19-year-old made a bright start by breaking serve in the first game. However, nerves appeared to get the better of her as she was swept aside 6-1, 6-2 by the diminutive Belgian who successfully claimed her third French title in a row.

The following year anxiety was far less of a problem for the attacking baseliner. Fresh from another Grand Slam final appearance in Melbourne, Ivanovic defeated Dinara Safina 6-4, 6-3 on Court Philippe Chatrier, becoming the first Serbian woman to win one of the Big Four. The following Monday she replaced Sharapova on the WTA rankings as the number one player in the world.

Ivanovic's form suffered following her victory in Paris and she quickly fell from the top spot, but an eighth career singles title towards the end of 2008 boded well for the future. A UNICEF ambassador boasting good looks and intelligence – she speaks three languages and is studying finance – one feels we haven't seen the last of Ana Ivanovic.

Jankovic

O ne of a flurry of eastern
Europeans to hit the big time,
Jelena Jankovic claimed the ultimate
prize of the number one spot in the
rankings on August 11 2008. The
achievement recognised an unbelievably
solid run during the first half of the
year – apart from Wimbledon, the
Serb reached at least the quarter-finals
of every tour event she entered.

But despite her undoubted ability,
nine tour wins and the fact she has
already bagged in excess of $6 million
in prize money, the 24-year-old has
so far disappointed in the tournaments
that really matter. In 2008 she reached
the semi-finals at the Australian Open
for the first time but was well beaten
by Maria Sharapova. Again, she made
the last four at Roland Garros, where
this time fellow Serb Ana Ivanovic
put paid to her hopes in three sets.

Following a fourth-round loss at
Wimbledon, Jankovic progressed
to her first ever Grand Slam final
at the US Open but was denied
by an inspired Serena Williams.

But it hasn't been all misery in the
Grand Slams for the likeable Serb who,
like Ivanovic is a UNICEF national
ambassador. In 2007 she won the hearts
of British fans by partnering Scotland's
Jamie Murray to the Wimbledon mixed
doubles crown.

▼ Jelena
Jankovic in
action at the
2008 Beijing
Olympics.

King

▶ Billie Jean King at full stretch.

▼ Billie Jean King with the Rosewater Dish, 1972.

Multiple Grand Slam champion, Fed Cup and Olympic tennis captain, businesswoman, author, commentator and campaigner for social change – Billie Jean King has been influential in numerous fields, and her efforts are still being recognised in sport and the world in general.

Born Billie Jean Moffitt on November 22 1943, the fearless net–rusher won 12 Grand Slam singles titles (including six Wimbledons and four US Opens). However, King was far from one–dimensional, picking up a further 16 ladies' doubles and 11 mixed doubles championships.

In fact, in 1973 the Californian took a rare "triple crown" at Wimbledon, winning the singles, doubles and mixed during the same fortnight. But, if it's possible, that year will be remembered for something even more spectacular – her victory over Bobby Riggs in the Battle of the Sexes.

Riggs, a former Wimbledon singles champion and accomplished showman, challenged King to a match, saying that, even at 55, he could beat the top women players. In a highly charged, televised exhibition game at the Houston Astrodome, King triumphed 6-4, 6-3, 6-3, striking what was seen by many as an important blow for equality in tennis and the wider social sphere.

Kournikova

Anna Kournikova is one of those rare sports stars who have become more famous for their appearance than their results. A marketer's dream, during the late 1990s and first few years of this century "Annamania" was rife – you were as likely to find images of the Moscow-born player in glossy magazines as in the newspaper sports pages.

It galled many tennis fans and commentators that Kournikova was so famous. During her brief career – she is semi-retired – she failed to win a singles tournament, with some claiming she epitomised "style over substance". But

such a straightforward summary is to do her a disservice.

A prodigiously gifted teenager, she reached the women's singles semi-final at Wimbledon aged just 16 where she was beaten by eventual champion Martina Hingis, and by November 2000 she was number eight in the world rankings. She twice won the Australian Open ladies' doubles championships and claimed 14 further pairs titles, at one point establishing herself as the number one doubles player on the planet.

Whatever anyone thinks of her, Kournikova was a phenomenon who drew attention to the game of tennis and brought a new legion of fans to the sport.

▲ Anna Kournikova hits a backhand.

◀ Adulation from fans follows Anna Kournikova wherever she plays.

Laver

▼ Rod Laver holding the trophy after winning at Wimbledon in 1969.

Two calendar year Grand Slams, 137 amateur singles titles, 47 professional championship victories. The greatest? Possibly.

A supreme athlete boasting a strong serve, powerful volleys and heavily top-spun groundstrokes on each side,

Rod Laver had it all. Able to adapt to any surface and vary his game with subtle spins Laver was a match for anyone in his day.

Born in Rockhampton, Queensland, Australia and christened "the Rocket" by the sporting press, Laver's most astonishing contributions to tennis lore were his two Grand Slams, one achieved as an amateur, the other as a pro.

In 1962, the then 23-year-old defeated great rival and compatriot Roy Emerson in the finals of the Australian Open, US Open and French Open, the last of these being a five set epic in which Laver was forced to recover from two sets down. Laver completed the set at Wimbledon with a 6-2, 6-2, 6-1 thrashing of fellow Australian Martin Mulligan.

Later that year Laver would turn professional and, as a result, be denied access to the Grand Slam tournaments until the "open" era began in 1968. But the 5ft 8in red-headed left-hander picked up where he left off in the paid ranks, establishing thrilling rivalries with yet another gifted Australian, Ken Rosewall, and the masterful Pancho Gonzales. During a highly successful paid career, Laver would win five US

◀ Rod Laver
making a
backhand return.

Pro titles and claim four consecutive victories at the prestigious London Pro Championships at Wembley.

Laver returned to Wimbledon in 1968 and claimed his fourth title at the All England with a straight sets victory over Tony Roche. The following year the Australian Open embraced the "open" concept, and Laver grasped the opportunity to become the first and, to date, only man to win a pro Grand Slam. Victories over Andres Gimeno, Rosewall, John Newcombe and Roche in the finals of the Big Four sealed the Rocket's legendary status. Laver was awarded the MBE in recognition of his achievements in 1970 but never again graced the final of a Grand Slam singles event.

Many forget that Laver was also a fine doubles player, partnering the likes of Emerson to six Grand Slam men's pairs titles, and was also on the winning side for Australia in five Davis Cup finals. All in all, he was the complete player, dominating the game for a decade. Better than Sampras or Federer? Unfortunately we'll never know for certain – let's just say he'd have given them a good game.

Left-Handers

▲ Left-handed
John McEnroe
playing a
forehand return.

Laver, McEnroe, Connors, Nadal. All great players, all ranked number one in the world and all left-handed.

In fact, compared with the ratio of right-handers to left-handers in the general population, when you take a look at the most famous names in tennis history, there does seem to be a disproportionate number of left-sided players in the men's game.

The great Rod Laver was a lefty, and during the early 1980s John McEnroe and Jimmy Connors virtually camped in the top three in the world, enjoying a spectacular rivalry with right-handed star Ivan Lendl.

Other big-name southpaws include Guillermo Vilas and former world number ones Marcelo Rios and Thomas Muster. Wimbledon champ Jaroslav Drobny was left-handed, as was multi Grand Slam winning Aussie, Tony Roche.

There are fewer female lefties to have claimed legendary status in the game. Martina Navratilova plays left-handed and many people's other candidate for the greatest female of all time, Margaret Court, was born a southpaw before switching to play right-handed.

Some believe left-handers have an advantage over righties. Not only are they unfamiliar opponents for orthodox opponents, they also have the opportunity to hit wide, swinging serves on arguably the most important points – at 30-40, 40-30 or on the advantage points.

Among the current crop of male tennis superstars, Rafael Nadal's name sticks out among the most gifted lefties, while in the women's game Patty Schnyder plays left-handed.

Lendl

Ninety-four singles titles, 1,071 of 1,310 professional matches won, 19 Grand Slam singles finals, 270 weeks at number one. Ivan Lendl posted

some pretty impressive numbers during his 16 years as a pro.

Of those 19 finals, the Czech-born athlete "only" managed to convert eight into victories – not a great success rate until you consider the quality of the opposition. Lendl's time in the spotlight came in an era graced by some of the finest talents ever to play the game, and his battles with the likes of Bjorn Borg, Jimmy Connors, John McEnroe, Mats Wilander and Boris Becker are legendary.

◄ Ivan Lendl in action, 1989.

Lendl, a hard-hitting, athletic baseliner, whose work ethic and steely determination defined the word "professional" in tennis, will be remembered by many British fans for his valiant efforts to add a Wimbledon title to his three French, three US and two Australian Open crowns.

The Czech – who later became a US citizen – reached the semi-finals on seven occasions between 1983 and '90 and progressed to the last two in '86 and '87 where he was defeated by Boris Becker and Pat Cash respectively. Many argue that Lendl, who tried so hard to adapt his game to the grass at SW19, is the finest player never to have won at the All England.

Lenglen

▶ Suzanne Lenglen in action at the 1920 Antwerp Olympics.

▼ Suzanne Lenglen at Wimbledon, 1922.

Suzanne Rachel Flore Lenglen was the first true female tennis superstar. Adored in her native France, Lenglen rose to fame in the 1920s and was something of a radical in that, during a time when women played in long restrictive skirts that touched the ground, she chose to don delicate dresses cut above the calf and which bared her forearms.

Renowned for her agility, Lenglen displayed almost balletic movements on the tennis court, often leaping full-stretched to retrieve the ball. And she used her athleticism to great effect, winning six Wimbledons, five of those consecutively, and remaining unbeaten at the All England. A French national champion, she also won the World Hard Court Championships, which were open to international competitors and played in Paris or Brussels, on four occasions. She is one of the few players to have claimed an Olympic gold medal, winning both the ladies' singles and mixed doubles in Antwerp in 1920.

A controversial character, she famously used to sip from a silver flask at end changes and was one of the first players to turn professional in 1926. Tragically Lenglen died of leukaemia just 12 years later at the age of 39.

McEnroe

The word "genius" is bandied around all too frequently nowadays but if there is one player worthy of that title in this book it is John Patrick McEnroe.

His unorthodox service action and forehand may not have sat easily with the purists, but McEnroe was blessed with incredible touch and a perhaps unmatched ability to disguise his shots. For all the world he may have looked as though he was going to hit a running backhand down the line, but a flick of the wrist would send the ball cross-court past a bemused opponent.

McEnroe burst into the international tennis consciousness at Wimbledon in 1977, when, as a slight 18-year-old, he came through qualifying and progressed to the semi-final of the main draw before going down to the great Jimmy Connors in four sets. "Mac" would

▲ John McEnroe's first outing at Wimbledon.

finally break Bjorn Borg's stranglehold on the championships four years later and he added two further titles with victories over Chris Lewis and Connors in the 1983 and '84 finals.

McEnroe was perhaps even more comfortable on the hard courts of the US Open. The home favourite triumphed on four occasions at Forest Hills, beating Vitas Gerulaitis in 1979, Borg in '80 and '81, and Ivan Lendl in '84. Mac's Grand Slam victories end there – he rarely played in the Australian

▲ John McEnroe
appeals against
the umpire's
decision.

▶ John McEnroe
with the men's
singles trophy,
Wimbledon,
1981.

Open and was never able to completely
come to terms with the slower clay
courts of Roland Garros, his best result
in Paris being a five-set defeat to Lendl
in the final of 1984. Interestingly, of
the great players faced by McEnroe
during his career, it was the Czech
who posed him the most problems.

Ranked number one in the world
for a total of 170 weeks at singles,
McEnroe was also an accomplished
doubles player, topping the pairs
rankings for 270 weeks. The 5ft 11in,
left-handed McEnroe was perfectly
complemented by 6ft 5in, right-handed
Peter Fleming and their partnership
secured seven Grand Slam doubles
titles as well as numerous crucial Davis
Cup victories.

But McEnroe's undeniable talent
came hand in hand with a notorious on-
court temper and "Super Brat", as he
became known, was as well known for
his outbursts against officialdom as his
sublime tennis. The American was even
disqualified in the fourth round of the
Australian Open in 1990 for persistent
bad behaviour.

Now a much-respected television
commentator, McEnroe continues to
thrill audiences on the seniors circuit.

Murray

Considering how much he has already achieved in the game, it's difficult to believe Andy Murray is still only 21.

Born in Dunblane, Scotland in 1987, Murray was hitting sponge balls against the wall by the age of three and proved he had the potential to rise to the very top when he claimed the prestigious Orange Bowl trophy in Miami at 12. By 17 he had played in his first Davis Cup match for Great Britain and the following year had won his first ATP Tour event. At the time of writing the Scot had just claimed his eighth title and was comfortably entrenched at number four in the world.

At one time commentators found fault with his fitness but Murray has silenced the critics in recent years with a new-found athleticism. His big breakthrough in terms of the Grand Slams came at Wimbledon in 2008 when he recovered from two sets down to defeat France's Richard Gasquet and reach the quarter-finals. Although soon-to-be-champion Rafael Nadal was too strong on this occasion, the Scot had his revenge on

the Spaniard a couple of months later in the semi-finals of the US Open with a mesmerising four-set victory.

The final against Roger Federer at Flushing Meadows proved a match too far for the young Scot, who is still aiming to become the first Briton since

▲ Andy Murray with one of his early trophies, 1999.

back victories in the Masters Series in Cincinnati and Madrid.

Predominantly an aggressive baseliner with an awesome counter-punch, Murray also has the ability to mix up his game and come to the net when necessary. Many believe his best chance of Grand Slam glory will come at Wimbledon, where enthusiastic supporters could help give him the edge. The Scot's predecessor Tim Henman certainly thrived with the home crowd behind him and there was evidence of "Murraymania" at SW19 during 2008.

▲ Andy Murray returns the ball.

▶ Andy Murray holds the trophy after his straight sets victory against Gilles Simon during the final of the 2008 Madrid Masters.

Fred Perry to win a Grand Slam event. Although Murray went into the match with a positive record against the Swiss star, he admitted afterwards that he had "a lot of improving to do if I want to win one of these tournaments".

Regardless of that disappointment, Murray enjoyed a spectacular 2008 – he had claimed five singles titles at the time of writing, including back-to-

Musketeers

In 1927 the unthinkable occurred and the French broke the American stranglehold on the Davis Cup. The players to pull off this remarkable achievement were Rene Lacoste, Henri Cochet, Jean Borotra and Jacques Brugnon – the legendary "Mousquetaires Francais" or French Musketeers.

Lacoste first put Bill Johnston to the sword before overcoming the great Bill Tilden in the reverse singles, while Cochet won one of his two singles rubbers to seal the deal at German Town Cricket Club in Philadelphia.

Such was the enormity of the achievement that the French authorities decided they needed a purpose-built arena for their defence of the title and Stade Roland Garros, now home of the French Open, was born. The French would hold the Cup for a further five years.

Each of the Musketeers achieved considerable success in his own right. Cochet won the French and US Championships and was a two-time Wimbledon champion, while the similarly prolific Lacoste went on to achieve fame for his tennis shirt designs which featured his famous "crocodile" logo. Borotra was the only one of the foursome to claim the Australian singles title while Brugnon, a doubles specialist, picked up the pairs titles in Australia, France and at Wimbledon.

▲ Two of the French Musketeers, Rene Lacoste and Jean Borotra in 1923.

▲▲ Henri Cochet in play at Wimbledon.

Nadal

N

◄ Rafael Nadal serving at the French Open, June 2008.

In 2008 Rafael Nadal achieved what many believe is the hardest of doubles, claiming back-to-back victories at the French Open and Wimbledon. The close proximity of the two tournaments and the fact they are played on such wildly different surfaces tests the stamina and versatility of the world's top players to the limit, and by winning both, the Spaniard emulated the likes of Rod Laver and Bjorn Borg. Nadal's victory in the French was his fourth in a row and his systematic 6-1, 6-3, 6-0 destruction of Roger Federer was a surprise to many. What came as even more of a shock was Nadal's victory over the Swiss player just a month later in one of the great Wimbledon finals. The Mallorcan-born baseliner swept to a two-set lead but Federer, bidding for a sixth consecutive victory at the All England,

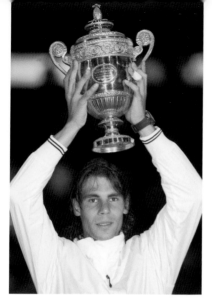

With his distinctive style – long hair, bandana, sleeveless shirt, knee-length shorts – and power game, Nadal has brought an extra touch of glamour to a game often criticised for producing uncharismatic sporting robots.

An individual though he is, Nadal is proud to play for his country. He helped Spain defeat America in the Davis Cup final of 2004 but was unable to take part in his country's historic victory over Argentina in the 2008 edition due to injury.

◀ Rafael Nadal with the 2008 Wimbledon trophy.

▼ Rafael Nadal in action at the Australian Open, 2008.

recovered to set up an astonishing final set. In approaching darkness, the tennis heavyweights traded blow after scintillating blow until, finally, Nadal broke the Federer serve and held his nerve to close out the match. The clearly overwhelmed Spaniard fell to the ground and we wondered whether this marked a changing of the guard.

After winning the gold medal at the Olympic Games in Beijing, Nadal ended a three-year wait as world number two behind Federer and claimed his place at the very top of the men's game.

Nastase

An icon to this day in his home country, Ilie Nastase put Romania on the tennis map during the 1970s, winning 57 titles, including the US Open of '72 and Roland Garros in '73.

A wonderfully stylish, all-court player, the Bucharest-born star possessed the deftest of touches as well as terrific speed. A charismatic entertainer with a vast array of shots and a strong sense of humour, Nastase could delight and dismay the tennis-watching public in equal measure. While much of his on-court horseplay was good-natured, his argumentative streak earned him the nickname "Nasty".

Despite his talent Nastase was unable to claim the Wimbledon crown, his best chance coming in 1972. Straightforward victories over a youthful Jimmy Connors in the quarter-finals and Spain's Manuel Orantes in the semis earned Nastase a final encounter with American number one seed Stan Smith. In what many believe was the finest ever Wimbledon final, Smith ultimately triumphed 4-6, 6-3, 6-3, 4-6, 7-5. The Romanian star would reach the final again in 1976 but he came up against Bjorn Borg at the beginning of his era of total domination on grass and, despite a spirited final set, Nastase succumbed 6-4, 6-2, 9-7.

THE LITTLE BOOK OF TENNIS

Navratilova

Tiger Woods, Annika Sorenstam, Michael Schumacher – very few can say they enjoyed complete domination of their chosen sport. Martina Navratilova is undoubtedly a member of that elite members' club for, during the 1980s, she held the tennis world in a vice-like grip.

Incredibly, between 1982 and '87 she reached 20 out of a possible 23 Grand Slam singles finals, winning 14 of them, including six consecutive Wimbledons. The finest of those years was undoubtedly 1984 when she enjoyed a record-breaking winning streak of 74 matches that lasted from January 20 to December 6.

And those incredible career stats keep on coming – a total of 167 singles titles, an 87% win rate, 331 weeks at number one.

Perhaps even more impressive than the numbers alone was Martina's longevity. Born in Prague, Czechoslovakia, on October 18 1956, the young Navratilova won her first main tour singles title in 1974. Her final tour title came an incredible 32 years later, when, at the age of 49

▲ Martina Navratilova after winning Wimbledon for the third time.

◄ Ilie Nastase at Wimbledon in 1975.

and 326 days, she won the US Open mixed doubles title with Bob Bryan and decided to finally hang up her racket. "I'm quitting because I want to, not because I have to," she said at the time.

By her retirement, Navratilova had completed the "boxed set" at the Grand Slams – that is she had won at least one title in singles, ladies' doubles and mixed doubles at each of the game's Majors. Her grand total of 59 Big Four wins included 18 singles victories and an unmatched 31 ladies' doubles titles, the

▲ Martina
Navratilova
hitting a return at
the French Open
in 1986.

▶ Martina
Navratilova
with her mixed
doubles partner
Bob Bryan in
2006.

majority of those achieved with Pam Shriver.

Granted US citizenship in 1981, Martina has unusually won the Fed Cup with two different countries. In 1975 she and Renata Tomanova led Czechoslovakia to a 3-0 victory over Australia in the final, while in '82 Navratilova teamed up with Chris Evert to beat Germany and claim the first of her Cups for the United States. In '86 she even helped the US to triumph against her former nation. In 2008, Navratilova announced that she had regained her Czech nationality and that she would hold dual citizenship.

A supporter of numerous charities, Martina has recently become involved in a fascinating project entitled Art Grand Slam, featuring artworks created by hitting paint-soaked balls onto canvas.

Noah

Yannick Noah's tennis career is defined by Roland Garros in 1983 when he became the first Frenchman to win on the Paris clay since 1946 when Marcel Bernard triumphed over Jaroslav Drobny.

Noah, a natural yet unorthodox player, was seeded six coming into the biggest tournament of his life, and he cruised his way through the draw to earn a quarter-final encounter with Ivan Lendl. Winning the first two sets 7-6, 6-2, the Frenchman let the third slip 7-5 but was then spurred into action, dispatching Lendl in the fourth

without losing a game.

An academic three-setter over fellow Frenchman Christophe Roger-Vasselin (the conqueror of number one seed Jimmy Connors), gave Noah his shot at the dream – a French Open final against defending champion Mats Wilander. Noah rose to the occasion and, in front of 17,000 ecstatic fans, earned himself legendary status with a 6-2, 7-5, 7-6 victory.

Noah would win the doubles crown with compatriot Henri Leconte the following year and, in 1991, captained his country to Davis Cup victory – France's first in 59 years. He led the French to the title again in 1996 and the following year was skipper of the women's team that claimed France's first ever Fed Cup. Now a highly successful musician, Noah has sold millions of albums worldwide.

◀ Yannick Noah on his way to winning the 1983 French Open.

▼ An agile Yannick Noah returning a serve.

Novotna

One of Wimbledon's most enduring images is of a distraught Jana Novotna crying on the shoulder of the Duchess of Kent following her defeat to Steffi Graf in the 1993 Wimbledon final.

Having led 4-1 in the final set against the German, the Czech athlete suffered a meltdown that allowed the defending champion back into the match. Graf capitalised and raced to a 7-6, 1-6, 6-4 victory and her fifth All England title. During the presentation ceremony it all became too much for Novotna when the Duchess said to her, "Don't worry Jana. You will win Wimbledon one day." The words were prophetic.

Novotna suffered another agonising final defeat to the then 16-year-old superstar, Martina Hingis, four years later but in 1998 she had her day. After dispatching Venus Williams in the quarters and gaining revenge on Hingis in the last four, Novotna came up against 16th seed Nathalie Tauziat on the final Saturday. In a battle of the serve and volleyers, the Czech finally triumphed 6-4, 7-6, laying the demons of '93 to rest and earning a standing ovation from the Centre Court crowd.

Perhaps an even better doubles player, Novotna won 12 Grand Slam ladies' pairs titles during her career and was on the victorious Fed Cup winning side of 1988.

THE LITTLE BOOK OF TENNIS

Number One

It is the dream of any professional sportsman or woman – to be the best in the world. But how do you measure "best"? In tennis, Grand Slam victories are often used to gauge a player's greatness but the other yardstick of a competitor's success is their position in the world rankings, with the number one spot the ultimate goal.

Where the ATP rankings are concerned, players are awarded points relative to their results in competitions ranging from elite Grand Slam championships to Challenger and Futures Tour events. The value of a result depends on the significance of the tournament entered – overall victory in a Grand Slam event is worth 200 points for example, while taking home the trophy in a Masters Series competition earns you 100, triumph in an International Series Gold tournament is valued at 60, and so on. A player's best 18 results (Grand Slams and Masters events are automatically counted) over a 52-week period count and each receives a weekly ranking – at the time of writing, Rafael Nadal was number one in the world with 6,675 points.

While the likes of Ilie Nastase, Jimmy Connors, Bjorn Borg, John

▲ Champions Jimmy Connors and Chris Evert with their Wimbledon trophies.

◀ At the end of 2008, Jelena Jankovic was world number one.

▲ Bjorn Borg who was one of the game's greats.

▶ The highly successful and versatile Roger Federer.

McEnroe, Ivan Lendl, Stefan Edberg, Pete Sampras and Roger Federer have all held the "official" number one spot since computer rankings were introduced, prior to the 1970s journalists were wont to compile their own ratings lists, with the likes of Bill Tilden, Pancho Gonzales and Ken Rosewall all crowned "number one".

The women's WTA Tour has a similar system and, again at the time of writing, Jelena Jankovic was ranked number one courtesy of two Grand Slam semi-finals, a runner-up spot at the US Open and four tournament victories in 2008. Steffi Graf holds the record on the women's tour for the longest unbroken spell at number one – an incredible 186 consecutive weeks between 1987 and 1990. Other legendary names to have graced the number one spot include Chris Evert, Martina Navratilova, Tracy Austin, Monica Seles, Arantxa Sanchez-Vicario, Martina Hingis, Lindsay Davenport, Venus Williams, and Belgian star Justine Henin, who retired in 2008 while still sitting at the top of the tree.

Both men's and women's tours also feature a season-long "race", points for which are calculated from results during the calendar year in question. The top eight players in any one year compete in an end-of-season big-money spectacular.

Oldies

It is impossible to do justice to all the great names of the past within these pages, but here we pay tribute to just a few of the players from days gone by who carved their place in tennis lore and helped shape the game we love today.

Spencer Gore was the first to make his mark in the fledgling sport of "lawn tennis" when he won the inaugural Wimbledon Championships in 1877. The Wimbledon Common-born 27-year-old, who also represented Surrey at cricket, came through the draw of 22 players to defeat William Marshall in straight sets. Ladies didn't play at the All England until 1884 when Maud Watson claimed the first of two consecutive Wimbledon titles, defeating her sister Lilian in the final.

William Renshaw was the first competitor to dominate the

▲ Spencer Gore, winner of the first Wimbledon tennis championship.

championships, winning six consecutive titles from 1881 to '86 – although it is important to note the presence of the Challenge round at the All England until 1921. At the same time on the other side of the pond, Richard Sears was in charge, claiming the first seven US Championships.

Other names of considerable note during the game's early years include Dorothea Lambert Chambers, who took

▲ Jack Kramer on Centre Court at Wimbledon.

▲▲ Jack Crawford wearing the attire of his day.

seven Wimbledon titles and would probably have won more had it not been for the intervention of the First World War. The charismatic Frenchwoman, Suzanne Lenglen, is remembered elsewhere in this book but the first truly global female superstar was Helen Wills Moody. The American won four French titles, seven US Championships and eight Wimbledons during her stellar career.

The Doherty brothers, Reginald and Lawrence (the latter of whom also broke the American stranglehold on the US Championships in 1903), and then the great New Zealander, Tony Wilding, dictated matters at Wimbledon prior to the War. Tragically Wilding was killed in the Battle of Aubers Ridge at Neuve Chappelle in 1915, aged just 31.

Between the wars Australia's Jack Crawford won the Australian, French and Wimbledon titles while the epic adventures of the French Musketeers are legendary. Post Second War, Jack Kramer established himself as the best player in the world, winning two US Championships and one Wimbledon. He went on to become a major success as a professional player and promoter and some think he may have been the best player of all.

Olympics

Oxford student John Boland travelled
to Athens to watch the 1896 Olympic
Games as a spectator but his friend
and secretary of the organising
committee Thrasyvoalos Manaos
entered him in the tennis event.
Apparently wearing leather street shoes,
the Irishman defeated all-comers to
become Olympic singles champion.
He teamed up with a German,
Freidrich Traun, to win doubles gold
too. How times have changed.

In 1988 tennis returned to the
Olympic Games in Seoul after a 64-
year hiatus. Open to fully-fledged
professionals, the graceful Miloslav
Mecir, came through the 64-strong
draw to win the men's singles and
Germany's Steffi Graf defeated Gabriela
Sabatini of Argentina in the women's
event. Meanwhile Ken Flach and
Robert Seguso joined Pam Shriver
and Zina Garrison as doubles gold
medallists, completing a pairs clean
sweep for the USA.

Tennis has remained as an Olympic
event ever since with Marc Rosset,
Jennifer Capriati, Andre Agassi, Lindsay
Davenport, Yevgeny Kafelnikov, Venus
Williams, Nicolas Massu, Justine Henin,
Rafael Nadal and Elena Dementieva
completing the list of modern-era
singles gold medallists.

To the delight of British fans,
Neil Broad and Tim Henman picked
up a doubles silver medal in 1996 in
Atlanta, losing in the final to legendary
pairing Todd Woodbridge and Mark
Woodforde of Australia.

▼ The medalists
on the podium
at the Beijing
Olympics.

Perry

British tennis viewers have grown accustomed to the phrase "… hoping to become the first British Wimbledon champion since Fred Perry in 1936". We hear it every year as the likes of Tim Henman or, more recently, Andy Murray, kick off their campaigns at SW19, attempting to emulate the Stockport player.

In fact Frederick John Perry won Wimbledon three times in a row between 1934 and '36, and clinched the Australian, US (three times) and French titles.

Perry was also instrumental in the 1933 victory over France that saw Britain bring home the Davis Cup for the first time in 21 years. While compatriot Bunny Austin sailed to a straightforward victory over Andre Merlin, it was Perry who displayed the wizardry in a thrilling five-set encounter against Musketeer Henri Cochet, eventually triumphing 8-10, 6-4, 8-6, 3-6, 6-1. Perry proved too strong for Merlin in the reverse singles and the Cup was on the boat home. The British, with Perry at the helm, would successfully defend the trophy on three occasions at Wimbledon.

Pin-Ups

Tennis has more than its fair share of "beautiful people" and ever since the game became popular, certain players have emerged as style, fashion and, indeed, sex icons.

In the 1920s Suzanne Lenglen dazzled the crowds with her controversial dress sense. Famed for her fur coats, silk, calf-length dresses and colourful headscarfs she was one of the most talked about stars of the day, a trendsetter adored by men and women alike.

Of course, times have changed and even Lenglen would have been shocked by some of the more revealing outfits on show today. The striking good looks of Chris Evert and Gabriela Sabatini turned heads during the 1970s and '80s, while, more recently, Anna Kournikova, Maria Sharapova and Ana Ivanovic have become the poster girls of a generation.

Of course, it's not just the women who raise the odd eyebrow. Ilie Nastase and John Newcombe were big favourites with the ladies during the 1970s, while Borg, Cash and Agassi attracted legions of admirers. The legendary battles between Boris Becker and Stefan Edberg at Wimbledon set some pulses racing for a variety of reasons while Rafael Nadal, Roger Federer and James Blake lead the way in the good looks brigade on the modern scene.

◀ Anna Kournikova looking glamorous on the tennis court.

▼ Bulging biceps and passion on court make Rafael Nadal one of the sport's pin-ups.

Prize Money

When Spencer Gore won the first ever Wimbledon men's singles title in 1877, he picked up 12 guineas for his trouble – a not insignificant amount of money at the end of the 19th century. However, that reward pales into insignificance compared with the pay cheques on offer for today's top players.

For example, the total prize money available at the US Open during 2008 amounted to more than $20 million, with the two singles champions – Roger Federer and Serena Williams – each picking up $1.5 million.

Of course, prize money at the Grand Slams has not always been awarded equally to men and women – for example, when Wimbledon opened up to professional players in 1968, Rod Laver received £2,000 for his tournament-winning efforts while Billie Jean King picked up just £750. Over the years players such as King campaigned for equal pay but it took until 2007 for Wimbledon and Roland Garros to fall in line with the Australian and US Opens and award identical payments from champions down to first-round losers.

In 2008 Roger Federer beat Pete Sampras' career earnings record, passing the $43 million mark.

Professionalism

Nowadays we take it for granted that players are rewarded financially for their efforts. But, as in the majority of sports, this has not always been the case. Right up until 1968 tennis was clearly split into two camps – the amateurs and the professionals – and objective judgements of players' "greatness" must always be tempered by the fact the two worlds rarely collided.

In 1926 the first professional tour was established by the sports promoter C C Pyle. The American signed up a "troupe" of celebrities to play in a series of exhibition matches at such prestigious venues as Madison Square Garden in New York and Boston Arena. The star attractions on this new circuit were former Wimbledon champion Suzanne Lenglen and American star Vincent Richards, who were well paid for their trouble.

Perhaps the most important name in the history of professionalism is the great Jack Kramer. A highly successful amateur, with Wimbledon and US Championships under his belt, the Las Vegas-born star turned pro at the end

▲ Suzanne Lenglen became a professional player in 1926.

of 1947 and embarked on a series of exhibition matches against Bobby Riggs and later Pancho Gonzales. In 1952 he turned promoter himself, recruiting the likes of Frank Sedgman, Ken Rosewall, Lew Hoad and Rod Laver.

As pros these great names were no longer able to play the Grand Slam events and it was only towards the end of the '60s that the pro-amateur divide was breached and the greatest players from both arenas finally mixed together.

Qualifying

▲ Gilles Muller made the quarter-final after qualifying for the US Open in 2008.

In the run-up to each glitzy Grand Slam tournament, another, equally hard-fought event takes place away from the media spotlight. This is the cauldron of frenetic activity that is "qualifying", from which a select few will emerge and claim a shot at the big time in the main draw.

Generally the top 104 players in the world automatically qualify for each of the Grand Slam events but there are another 24 places to be filled by qualifiers and wildcards. Unlike a normal tournament draw there is no overall "winner" in qualifying. For example, at the Australian Open in 2008, 128 players were entered in the men's singles qualifying draw, from which 16 progressed to the main event, including Britain's Jamie Baker.

Over the years qualifiers have achieved considerable success. In 1977, for example, a then 18-year-old John McEnroe came through the prelims and made it all the way to the Wimbledon semi-final before being defeated in four sets by Jimmy Connors. And in 2008 at the US Open, Gilles Muller, then ranked 130 in the world, came through qualifying and was only defeated at the quarter-final stage by eventual champion Roger Federer.

Queen's

The week after the French Open many of the best players in the world congregate at The Queen's Club in West Kensington, London, for the second most famous grass court tournament of them all. Following the conclusion of a 30-year association with Stella Artois, the event became the AEGON Championships in 2009.

Regardless of its name, Queen's is traditionally held a fortnight before Wimbledon and gives players the ideal opportunity to adjust from the slow clay of Roland Garros to the faster grass surface. Over the years it has produced some magnificent champions, many of whom have used it as a springboard to victory at the All England. Jimmy Connors (1982), John McEnroe ('81, '84), Pete Sampras ('95, '99), Lleyton Hewitt (2002) and Rafael Nadal ('08) have all done the Queen's–Wimbledon double but perhaps the most famous achiever of this feat was Boris Becker.

The Queen's Club, established in 1886 and named after Queen Victoria, is famously home to a variety of racket sports and contains two real tennis courts within its extensive grounds.

▲ No 1 Court at Queen's.

Queues

▲ Spectators
queue up
to enter
Wimbledon.

▶ A queue on
People's Sunday
at Wimbledon.

Tennis fans are a hardy bunch and the sight of snaking queues around the All England Club during Wimbledon is common on our television screens.

So desperate are some Wimbledon fans to see their idols that they choose to camp in the queue overnight in the hope of securing one of the coveted show court tickets available each day at the turnstiles. The All England is so used to this practice that it issues "queue cards" showing each person's

position, and it has even produced a "Code of Conduct" outlining queuing etiquette. For example, you are not permitted to reserve a place for somebody else and leaving equipment unattended is prohibited.

Huge queues often correspond with interest in British players and record numbers waited in line on the first Friday in 2001 with the prospect of both Tim Henman and Greg Rusedski appearing on Centre Court.

As well as 500 tickets for Centre, No 1 and No 2 courts (apart from on the last four days), in the region of 6,000 ground passes are available to queuers each day. Once the club reaches its safety capacity of 36,000, spectators are admitted on a one-in, one-out basis.

86   THE LITTLE BOOK OF TENNIS

Racket

E ver since players decided it would be more fun to hit a ball with something other than their hand, the race to develop the perfect racket has been on.

First a wooden paddle and then a wooden, stringed frame were produced. In fact wood, principally ash, continued to dominate the scene right through to the 1970s but the success of players such as Jimmy Connors and his steel Wilson T2000 racket spelled the beginning of the end for the traditional material. Following steel, aluminium became the metal of choice but nowadays most rackets are made of strong carbon fibre composites.

Following technological advances, the International Tennis Federation decided to limit the parameters of rackets. There are strict rules on permitted stringing patterns and size of

▲ Racket makers in the 1930s.

"hitting surface" and the frame must not be longer than 73.7cm or wider than 31.7cm.

Over the years the general shape of the tennis racket has changed little although various innovations have been tried. From the "fishtail" grips of the late 1800s and early 1900s, to models with offset heads, wide bodies and even double handles, manufacturers are constantly innovating in the search for the perfect weapon.

top of their games.

When looking at famous rivalries in the men's game, one name appears again and again – the charismatic John McEnroe, who enjoyed a series of famous showdowns with Jimmy Connors, Bjorn Borg and, ultimately, Ivan Lendl.

Although the pair only met 14 times, fiery, bad-tempered McEnroe and glacial Borg were the perfect sparring partners. The American serve-volleyer

Rivalries

▲ Rivals John McEnroe and Jimmy Connors.

▶ Martina Navratilova and Chris Evert battled it out for 16 years.

Fighting it out on a court measuring 8m by 24m, often surrounded by high, banked stands containing thousands of excited spectators, the modern tennis gladiator is the ultimate entertainer. Occasionally the spectacle is heightened by the presence of two true rivals, players who have battled it out for a number of years, each at the very

got the better of the top-spinning baseliner in terms of Grand Slam finals, beating Borg in two US Open finals and once at Wimbledon. The pair are probably best remembered for Borg's victory in the Wimbledon final of 1980 when the Swede claimed his fifth consecutive title in one of the best matches ever played.

Against Connors, McEnroe enjoyed a 20-14 win/loss record over the course of 14 years. However, they only met in two Grand Slam finals, sharing the spoils at Wimbledon.

Lendl was the only man to get the better of Supermac, defeating him in a classic 1984 French Open final and the '85 final at the US Open. McEnroe's sole Grand Slam singles final win over Lendl came at Flushing Meadows in 1984 and he lost their career battle 21-15.

In the ladies' game, Martina Navratilova and Chris Evert's 16-year duel is documented elsewhere in this book but the Czech-American had another formidable adversary in Germany's Steffi Graf. When the pair first met in 1985, Navratilova had already been at the top of the ladies' game for seven years and Martina would win their first three encounters with ease.

▲ Rafael Nadal and Roger Federer, the latest emerging rivals.

However, a 6-2, 6-3 victory for the German on home turf the following year signalled the beginning of a fierce contest that included six Grand Slam finals. Although Graf won four of those six big finals, over the course of their careers it was honours even, nine matches apiece.

One fascinating rivalry that seems to be emerging is between Roger Federer and Rafael Nadal. Still at the peak of their games, the Spaniard enjoys a 12-6 advantage at the time of writing.

Roddick

▲ Andy Roddick seems to be a permanent fixture in the world's top 10.

Andrew Stephen Roddick, or "A-Rod" as he's been dubbed, seems to have been on our screens forever, yet he's still only 26. Seemingly a permanent fixture in the world's top 10, the big-serving right-hander from Nebraska briefly claimed the number one spot in the rankings at the end of 2003.

Despite his highly successful career – he had won 26 singles titles and more than $14 million in prize money at the time of writing – Roddick has just one Grand Slam on his CV. His finest hour came at the 2003 US Open, where, after a five-set tussle with David Nalbandian of Argentina in the semis, he cruised to victory over Spanish star Juan Carlos Ferrero, 6-3, 7-6, 6-3. As an emotional Roddick celebrated in front of a delighted home crowd, we all wondered how many more Big Four wins would come his way. To date none – and that is largely down to a certain Swiss star. Roger Federer defeated A-Rod in the 2004 and '05 Wimbledon finals, and disappointed him yet again the following year at Flushing Meadows.

The proud possessor of the fastest ever recorded serve – a 155mph rocket fired at Vladimir Voltchkov of Belarus in a 2004 Davis Cup tie – Roddick has played 40 matches in the international team competition and was on the winning side in 2007.

Runner-Up

The famous trophy is handed over and the champion kisses it before embarking on a celebratory lap of the court, waving to the crowd, dazzled by a thousand flashbulbs. To the victor the spoils. But unfortunately there is always another player, sat disconsolately in his or her chair, trying to take in the magnitude of what has just happened.

Historically, most of the biggest names have had a "bogey" tournament – the likes of John McEnroe, Pete Sampras and, to date, Roger Federer have been unable to conquer the clay at Roland Garros and Ilie Nastase, Ken Rosewall and Ivan Lendl are famous for never having won Wimbledon.

But who are the best players never to have won a Grand Slam singles

title? In the modern era, the likes of Miloslav Mecir, the supremely gifted Slovak athlete, and America's Todd Martin, both of whom lost Australian and US Open singles finals, spring to mind. And what about France's Henri Leconte, defeated by Mats Wilander at Roland Garros in 1988? In the women's game one name that sticks out is that of Helena Sukova. The Czech athlete reached the Australian Open finals of 1984 and '89, losing to Chris Evert and Steffi Graf respectively, and the last two at Flushing Meadows in 1986 and '93, where Martina Navratilova and Graf again spoiled her party.

◀ A disconsolate Todd Martin on his way to losing against Goran Ivanisevic at Wimbledon.

▼ Henri Leconte (right) with the runner-up trophy at Roland Garros.

Rusedski

▲ Canadian born Greg Rusedski flying the flag for Britain.

▶ Power server Greg Rusedski in action.

When Greg Rusedski decided he wanted to be a British citizen in 1995, few could have imagined the impact he would have on the nation's tennis scene.

Born in Montreal in 1973, Rusedski won the Canadian junior championships and reached the world's top 50 before heading across the pond to compete for Britain. He immediately made an impact in the Davis Cup, winning both his singles rubbers against Monaco and kick-starting GB's rise from the doldrums of Euro/African Group II. In total, Rusedski played 43 matches in the competition, winning 30, and it was fitting that he would finally call a halt to his tennis career at the event following a triumphant appearance against the Netherlands.

But Rusedski's career is about far more than team tennis. The winner of 15 singles titles, his finest hour came in 1997 when he went one further than compatriot and rival Tim Henman by reaching the final of a Grand Slam event – the US Open. Although Rusedski was beaten 6-3, 6-2, 4-6, 7-5 by Pat Rafter of Australia, the effort helped him reach his career-high ranking of fourth in the world.

Rusedski will be best remembered for his enormous left-handed serve, at one time the fastest in the world.

Russians

At the time of writing an incredible five of the women's top 10 and 11 of the top 50 female players in the world were Russian.

The eastern European country has always produced strong competitors but global domination began in 2004. At Roland Garros, two Russians met in a Grand Slam final for the first time in tennis history as Anastasia Myskina defeated Elena Dementieva 6-1, 6-2.

The floodgates had been opened and a few weeks later Maria Sharapova outplayed Serena Williams on the grass to win Wimbledon. The perfect end to Russia's year came at Flushing Meadows as the unfortunate Dementieva was again defeated, this time by compatriot Svetlana Kuznetsova.

Things have calmed down a little since but Sharapova has added two more Grand Slam singles titles to her CV and the likes of Dinara Safina (who was ranked number three in the world at the close of 2008) and Kuznetsova have also reached finals.

While the men cannot boast quite such impressive strength in depth,

players such as Nikolay Davydenko, Igor Andreev, Dmitry Tursonov and former US and Australian Open champion Marat Safin are flying the flag for Russia at the top end of the ATP Tour.

▲ The two successful Russians at Roland Garros in 2004, Anastasia Myskina and Elena Dementieva.

◀ Marat Safin, has won two Grand Slam singles titles .

Sampras

A genuine contender for the "best ever" tag, Pete Sampras was the most outstanding player of the 1990s, winning 14 Grand Slam singles titles and spending 286 weeks at number one.

A genuine all-court player, Sampras was most at home at Wimbledon, where he claimed seven singles titles, the last four consecutively. The key to his success on the grass of SW19 was a metronomic, accurate serve and his ability to return the best his opponents could throw at him – with interest.

Sampras first entered the public consciousness in 1990 when he became the youngest ever US Open singles winner. Aged just 19, the number 12 seed defeated such luminaries as Ivan Lendl and John McEnroe on his way to the final where he came up against the man who would become his greatest rival – Andre Agassi. Sampras' 6-4, 6-3, 6-2 victory was the first of three over the Las Vegan at Flushing Meadows.

During his career "Pistol" Pete bagged 64 singles titles but one championship continued to evade him. Despite 13 attempts on the clay of Roland Garros, his best result was a semi-final appearance in 1996, where he went down in straight sets to Russia's Yevgeny Kafelnikov.

Sanchez

Spain's Sanchez family has arguably the strongest tennis-playing gene pool of them all, for during the 1980s and '90s it produced three world class competitors, the most famous of whom was Arantxa Sanchez-Vicario.

Arantxa, who was known on tour by her family name of Sanchez-Vicario, turned pro in 1985 and four years later claimed her first Grand Slam at the French Open, defeating number one seed Steffi Graf in the final. She would win twice more on her favoured clay

surface at Roland Garros and added a victory in the US Open in 1994. Ranked number one at singles, she simultaneously claimed the top spot at doubles in 1995. A tenacious competitor with wonderful touch she helped her country to five Fed Cup victories.

Although he was ranked as high as seventh at singles, elder brother Emilio was also something of a pairs specialist, winning the men's and mixed doubles titles at both the French and US Opens. The third Sanchez to forge a successful career on the tennis court was Javier, who reached number 23 at singles and was ranked top 10 at doubles.

◀ Arantxa Sanchez-Vicario of Spain, 1994.

◀◀ Pete Sampras was the youngest ever men's champion at Flushing Meadows.

▼ Emilio Sanchez reached a career high of seventh in the world.

Seles

Expelling distinctive grunts of exertion as she bludgeoned double-handed forehands and backhands from the back of the court, Monica Seles was the first of a new breed of power hitters to descend on the women's tour.

But the Yugoslav-born Seles was more than just a powerhouse.

Displaying phenomenal accuracy and fast footwork, she also had a great tennis brain. This impressive combination led her to the French Open title at just 16 years six months and she would win a further seven Grand Slam titles over the next three years.

Despite her dominance, she was never completely at home on the grass courts of

Wimbledon and reached the final just once in 1992 where she was defeated by great rival Steffi Graf.

Sadly the on-court contest with Graf led to one of the most horrific sports news stories of the 20th century when a fanatical supporter of the German stabbed Seles in the back during a match in 1993. Seles would not return to the competitive arena for more than two years and never quite recovered her scintillating form of old, although she did claim a final Grand Slam event – the Australian Open of 1996.

Seles, who became an American citizen in 1994, struggled with a foot injury later in her career and played her last competitive match in 2003.

Sharapova

When Maria Sharapova defeated Lindsay Davenport and then Serena Williams to win Wimbledon in 2004 at the age of 17, a star was born.

Towering over most of the opposition at 6ft 2in and boasting movie star looks, the Russian has taken the world by storm, earning more than $12 million before her 22nd birthday – and that's just in prize money. After her triumph at SW19, Sharapova lost out in five Grand Slam semi-finals but any thoughts that she might have been a one-hit wonder were dispelled at the 2006 US Open. There she defeated Justine Henin 6-4, 6-4 in the final at Flushing Meadows with a fearsome display of serving power.

In 2008 she added to her Grand Slam set with victory in Melbourne over Ana Ivanovic, leaving just the French Open missing from her CV. Her best result on the slower clay surface to date is a semi-final appearance against Ivanovic in 2007.

Sharapova struggled with a shoulder injury during 2008 and had slipped down the rankings at the time of writing.

◀ Maria Sharapova poses with the trophy after victory at the Australian Open, 2008.

▼ Maria Sharapova and Serena Williams walk on to Centre Court for the start of the 2004 Wimbledon final.

Spanish Stars

▲ Tommy Robredo has won nine singles titles.

David Ferrer, Fernando Verdasco, Nicolas Almagro, Tommy Robredo… the list goes on. Boasting more male players in the world's top 50 than any other country at the time of writing, Spain is vying with France for the title of "strongest nation in tennis". What's more they have the number one player on the planet – Rafael Nadal.

Traditionally strongest on clay courts, the Spanish men have dominated at Roland Garros in recent years. The tone was set by Sergi Bruguera's back-to-back victories in 1993 and '94, Carlos Moya added to the tally in '98 and between 2002 and '08 a Spanish run of victories was broken just once as Albert Costa ('02), Juan Carlos Ferrero ('03) and Nadal ('05-'08) made their marks.

But for Spain's first champion at Roland Garros you need to go back to 1961 and Manuel Santana. The great "Manolo" defeated Nicola Pietrangeli in the final that year and went on to do the double over the Italian three years later. Not content with clay court excellence, Santana won two further Grand Slam singles titles on grass – the US Championships of 1965 and Wimbledon in '66. Manolo also led Spain to their first ever Davis Cup final in '65, although his side would eventually lose 4-1 to the mighty Australians.

Since then Spain have reached a further five finals of tennis' most prestigious team competition. They claimed their first victory in 2000, Ferrero defeating Patrick Rafter and Lleyton Hewitt, and Juan-Manuel Balcells and Alex Corretja teaming up to win the doubles over Australia. The

Spanish won again in 2004 and in '08 made it three, triumphing 3-1 over home side Argentina.

The Spanish women's team also had plenty to shout about during the 1990s as Arantxa Sanchez-Vicario and Conchita Martinez spearheaded an assault on the Fed Cup that resulted in five victories. In fact Spain made the final as recently as 2008 courtesy of Nuria Llagostera Vives, Anabel Medina Garrigues and Carla Suarez Navarro.

While not setting the singles rankings alight Medina Garrigues reached number 22 in 2008 and Suarez Navarro – still only 20 years old – broke into the top 50. The pair have some way to go to emulate Sanchez-Vicario, who won nine Grand Slam singles titles, and Martinez, who defeated Martina Navratilova on the grass of Wimbledon back in 1994.

▲ Manuel Santana in action at Wimbledon.

◀ Anabel Medina Garrigues is a picture of concentration.

Superstitions

There aren't many ladders to walk under or black cats to avoid on the pro tour but the top players have come up with their own idiosyncratic ways of coping with the pressures of competitive tennis.

Perhaps the most famously superstitious player was Goran Ivanisevic who had a series of rituals he followed during Wimbledon fortnight. Not only did he eat the same meal at the same restaurant each day but, in 2001, he watched the *Teletubbies* prior to each match for luck. It clearly paid off for the Croat, who claimed his sole Grand Slam singles success at SW19 that year.

And Tim Henman, who lost to Ivanisevic in the semi-finals, said he always used the same shower cubicle after a match.

But it's not just the men who rely on more than their playing skills for success. Australia's Jelena Dokic once said she wore the same clothes at the All England for each match – hand washing them each day – and even Venus Williams has confessed to having lucky dresses.

Bjorn Borg wouldn't shave while he was winning while John McEnroe had lucky socks earlier in his career and, like current women's star Ana Ivanovic, had a thing about walking on the lines of the court.

Surfaces

Not only do tennis players have to master all the strokes and the complexities of the tactical and mental games, but they have to learn to cope with a variety of playing surfaces. Each type of court has its own characteristics and, as a result, surface specialists tend to emerge.

Up until 1974 three of the four Grand Slam tournaments – the Australian Open, Wimbledon and US Open – were played on grass courts but in '75 the American Championships joined Roland Garros by introducing a clay surface.

In 1978, the US event moved to Flushing Meadows and the courts were changed again – this time to a hard surface.

Ten years later the Australian Open also adopted hard courts and nowadays both these prestigious tournaments are played on acrylic.

The French Open is, of course, the sole Grand Slam event to be played on clay courts nowadays. Renowned for its slow playing characteristics and fine,

▲ The Plexicushion surface in Melbourne.

▲ Roland Garros' clay courts.

▶ Wimbledon is the only Grand Slam event now played on grass.

grainy top layer which allows players to slide into their shots, clay creates a game within a game. Favouring baseline players and placing a high premium on accuracy, consistency and endurance, some notable clay court exponents have emerged over the years. To date Rafael Nadal is unbeaten at Roland Garros on the surface and the court texture seems to appeal to the Spanish stars in general. Another player to dominate in the dusty red Parisian arena in recent times is Brazil's Gustavo Kuerten, who claimed the trophy in 1997, 2000 and '01.

Just a fortnight after the French Open concludes, the players are forced to adapt their games to an entirely different surface – the natural grass of Wimbledon, where the ball skids much more quickly off the ground and the bounce is generally lower. In the past, serve and volleyers such as John McEnroe, Pat Cash and Boris Becker tended to have an advantage but in recent years it is generally agreed that the grass of SW19 has slowed.

Away from the Grand Slams the list of types of court is never ending with surfaces ranging from porous asphalt (popular in clubs across the UK) to artificial grass (the speed of which can be altered by the addition or removal of sand), polymeric material and even fast wood boards.

Tie-Break

In 1969 Pancho Gonzales took five hours and 12 minutes to defeat Charlie Pasarell in the first round at Wimbledon. The final score was 22-24, 1-6, 16-14, 6-3, 11-9, the pair having played an incredible 112 games of tennis. Although this was an extraordinary occurrence, lengthy matches were commonplace and the authorities decided something needed to be done to shorten games and retain spectators' interest. The result was the tie-break, an early version of which was introduced at the 1970 US Open.

Wimbledon adopted the idea the following year (although tie-breaks were played at 8-8) and in 1979 the version we know today was put in play at the All England. While men's singles matches are still the best of five sets, in each of the first four sets a tie-break is played if the score reaches 6-6.

Players serve alternately for two points (although the player who serves first does so just once at the outset of the tie-break) and the winner is the first to reach seven, provided they are two clear points ahead (7-5, 8-6 etc).

In the final set at Wimbledon there is no tie-break and players are required to win by two clear games as was exemplified in the 2008 final where Rafael Nadal defeated Roger Federer 6-4, 6-4, 6-7, 6-7, 9-7.

▲ Pancho Gonzales takes a breather during his marathon match against Charlie Pasarell.

▼ Scoreboard showing that the third set went to a tie-break.

Tilden

▲ Bill Tilden, one of the greatest players of his time.

▶ Tilden was renowned for his groundstrokes.

"Big Bill" Tilden was undoubtedly the biggest name in amateur tennis during the 1920s, and during that decade won three Wimbledon titles as well as seven US Championships, six of those consecutively. The possessor of a thunderbolt service and a versatile master of the back-court game, Tilden was the lynchpin of the United States Davis Cup team, leading his country to victory and six successive defences between 1920 and '26.

But as well as being one of the greatest ever exponents of the game, Tilden was a controversial character.

Loved by many but seen as arrogant and rude by others, he was often at odds with the tennis establishment and caused a major stir in the late 1940s when he was twice imprisoned, once on a morals charge, the other for a parole violation.

Despite his turbulent private life, Tilden was the first, highly successful professional tennis player, drawing in as many as 16,000 spectators to venues such as Madison Square Garden in New York as he embarked on a celebrated 1934 tour with the great Ellsworth Vines.

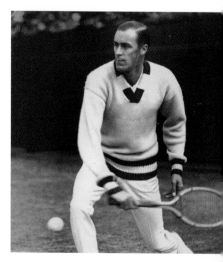

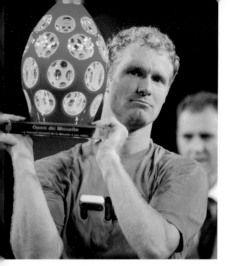

Trophies

Apart from the huge pay cheques that inevitably accompany tournament victories on the major men's and women's tours, it's the trophies the players are after. The Grand Slam ones are the most special, steeped as they are in decades of history, while others are of particular interest due to their shape, size or value.

One of the most impressive winner's cups in world sport is the Wimbledon men's singles trophy. Standing 18.5in high and with a diameter of 7.5in, the silver gilt masterpiece bears the intriguing inscription "The All England Lawn Tennis Club Single Handed Champion of the World". The ladies' champion receives the beautiful Venus Rosewater Dish, first presented in 1886. Decorated with mythical characters, the silver salver is a copy of a pewter work in the Louvre.

The French Open men's singles champion is handed the Coupe des Mousquetaires while the ladies hold the Coupe Suzanne Lenglen aloft. In Melbourne the victors get to kiss the Norman Brookes Challenge Cup or the Daphne Akhurst Memorial Cup.

One trophy most players would love to have on their mantelpiece is the tennis racket Amelie Mauresmo was allowed to keep in 2007 for winning the Diamond Games in Belgium three times in a row. Made of gold and studded with 1,702 diamonds, it was worth an estimated $1.3 million!

◀ Tennis trophies come in all shapes and sizes. This is the Moselle Open trophy.

▼ Venus Williams with the Venus Rosewater Dish.

Tsonga

Jo-Wilfried Tsonga was a relative unknown when he astounded the tennis-watching public with his 6-2, 6-3, 6-2 demolition of Rafael Nadal at the 2008 Australian Open. Ranked 38 in the world at the time, the Le Mans-born Frenchman could do no wrong as he raced to victory in 117 minutes and sealed his place in the final against Novak Djokovic. There was no repeat performance on the second Sunday as

the Serbian recovered from a one-set deficit to claim the Norman Brookes Challenge Cup, but in Tsonga a new star had been born.

"Ali", as he is affectionately known due to his resemblance to the boxing great, earned his revenge against Djokovic in Bangkok later in the year and then claimed his biggest win to date by defeating David Nalbandian in the final of the ATP Masters Series Paris competition. Tsonga came back from three break points down as he served for the final set, and the tears flowed freely as he finally triumphed 6-3, 4-6, 6-4.

Ranked a career-high sixth in November, it remains to be seen whether the 6ft 2in powerhouse can step up a final level and claim a first Grand Slam title.

Umpire

To become a world class tennis umpire takes years of dedication, experience and numerous qualifications but the hard work is repaid with the opportunity to travel the globe and become involved in world class sport.

The first step towards becoming a fully fledged international "chair umpire" is to become a "line umpire". When you have gained some experience calling lines you can attend further courses and eventually become an International Tennis Federation White Badge Official. There is then the opportunity to upgrade your status to Bronze, Silver or Gold Badge "international chair umpire" under the ITF scheme.

As well as announcing the scores between points, the chair umpire needs to have strong people and crowd control skills, an encyclopaedic

▲ The umpire tosses a coin at the start of a match between Marat Safin and Roger Federer.

knowledge of the rules and the ability to pronounce correctly everything from Amanmuradova to Zverev. He or she is also responsible for making critical decisions such as whether a court remains fit for play.

Perhaps most importantly of all, the very best umpires have to have a cool head – not easy when a superstar is yelling at you in front of a crowd of thousands and potentially millions of television viewers!

US Open

▲ Crowds at the
US Open.

Second only to Wimbledon in terms of longevity, America's Grand Slam tournament has been in existence since 1881. Originally a men's event reserved solely for members of United States Lawn Tennis Association affiliated clubs, the inaugural singles championship was played at Newport Casino in Rhode Island, where Richard Sears claimed the first of seven consecutive titles.

The US men's and ladies' singles and doubles events, as well as the mixed doubles, have visited nine different venues over the years but the most famous hosts have been West Side Tennis Club in Forest Hills and current home, the USTA Billie Jean King National Tennis Center in Flushing Meadows, New York.

The US Championships became "Open" in 1968 at Forest Hills, when amateurs and professionals competed alongside each other for the first time. The singles winners that year were Arthur Ashe and Virginia Wade but, due to his amateur status, Ashe, a lieutenant in the army, was only entitled to $20 expenses while the Englishwoman picked up a winner's cheque for $6,000. Ashe was paid the ultimate tribute when the principal new show court at Flushing Meadows was opened bearing his name in 1997.

Attracting more than 700,000 spectators at the end of August, the US Open is the star-spangled climax to the Grand Slam season and the honour roll is littered with legendary names. Bill Tilden shares the accolade of having won the most men's singles titles with Sears (seven) but Big Bill's 91% win rate at the championship is unsurpassed. Molla Bjurstedt Mallory took the ladies' singles eight times between 1915 and '26, while Chris Evert made the event her own in the late '70s and early '80s with six victories. In 2008, Roger Federer further boosted his legendary status at the US Open, grabbing a fifth consecutive title in a straight-sets final victory over Britain's Andy Murray.

▼ Roger Federer claimed his fifth US Open title in a row in 2008.

Veterans

▶ John McEnroe continues to entertain the crowds.

▼ Veteran Bjorn Borg in action.

One of the beauties of tennis is that you can go on playing it well into later life (there is an International Tennis Federation Seniors world ranking list for over-85s!) and although your speed around the court may diminish, a player's touch sometimes improves with age.

At Wimbledon, invitational tournaments for players who are no longer regulars on the main tours are very popular, giving spectators the opportunity to watch their old heroes. The likes of Pat Cash, Wayne Ferreira, Guy Forget, Cedric Pioline and the famous Woodies could be seen playing in the Gentlemen's Invitation Doubles in 2008, while Henri Leconte, Vijay Amritraj, Anders Jarryd and Guillermo Vilas competed in the Senior men's doubles. Similarly, Hana Mandlikova, Jana Novotna, Nathalie Tauziat, Conchita Martinez, Helena Sukova and the great Martina Navratilova fought it out in the ladies' invitation doubles.

The "Legends" doubles at the Australian Open was won in 2008 by Wayne Arthurs and Richard Fromberg, while John Alexander and Rachel McQuillan took the mixed. There are similar events at the French and US Opens while London's Royal Albert Hall regularly plays host to seniors tennis events showcasing the likes of John McEnroe and Ilie Nastase.

Victory!

The euphoria of victory is hard to match – and tennis has seen its fair share of ecstatic celebration over the years. Wimbledon fans will never forget Bjorn Borg dropping to his knees in 1980, Becker's arms aloft in '85, Andre Agassi prostrate on the ground after his 1992 triumph over Goran Ivanisevic or the Croatian's tears of joy at finally clinching the title nine years later.

In fact Ivanisevic's countrymen

◀ Who can forget Bjorn Borg's five in a row at Wimbledon.

enjoyed the victory as much as the big-serving left-hander, treating him to a hero's welcome on his return to his homeland. It is estimated that 150,000 people turned up to cheer him as he arrived in Split's harbour by boat 24 hours after his historic win.

But if there is any event bound to set the national pulse racing, it is the Davis Cup. There were scenes of jubilation in 1991 when France won the famous trophy for the first time in 59 years and as 2008 drew to a close, Spain clinched their third Davis Cup victory, sparking wild celebration from players and their supporters.

◀ Goran Ivanisevic celebrates as he wins at Wimbledon in 2001.

Vive La France!

With an incredible 14 players in the
men's top 100 at the end of 2008 and
11 in the women's upper echelons,
France is a hotbed of tennis talent.

And not since 1988 and the days
of Yannick Noah and Henri Leconte
had the nation boasted two male
players in the world's top 10. Jo-
Wilfried Tsonga and Gilles Simon
both had a phenomenal 2008, the
former reaching his first Grand Slam
singles final and Simon claiming singles
titles in Casablanca, Indianapolis and
Bucharest. But it didn't stop there.
Aged just 21, Gael Monfils became the
first Frenchman in 10 years to reach
the semi-finals at Roland Garros, and
France had four more top-50 stars in
Richard Gasquet, Paul-Henri Mathieu,
Michael Llodra and Julien Benneteau by
the close of the season.

Yet despite their impressive
strength in depth, the French men
are suffering a win-drought where
the Grand Slams are concerned. This
is largely down to the dominance of
two men. Switzerland's Roger Federer
and Rafael Nadal of Spain have had
something of a stranglehold on the Big
Four in recent years and Noah remains
the last Frenchman to win a Major
title, courtesy of his Roland Garros
triumph in 1983.

THE LITTLE BOOK OF TENNIS

The women have had no such trouble. Mary Pierce was victorious in Melbourne in 1995, and in 2000 delighted a nation by becoming the first home female player to win the French Open since Francoise Durr in 1967. Amelie Mauresmo then took up the baton, claiming the Australian Open and Wimbledon in 2006 and claiming the top spot in the world rankings. Although she has since slipped outside the top 20, Alize Cornet and Marion Bartoli were ranked 16 and 17 at the end of 2008.

Of course no summary of French tennis is complete without mention of the Davis Cup and the French share the honour with Great Britain of being the third-most decorated nation in the competition. The exploits of the "Mousquetaires" in the 1920s and '30s are documented elsewhere in this book but France have claimed momentous victories in 1991, '96 and, most recently, 2001 courtesy of the likes of Nicolas Escude, Sebastian Grosjean and the doubles pairing of Cedric Pioline and Fabrice Santoro, otherwise known as "The Magician". Not to be outdone, the French ladies have two Fed Cup victories to their

name, their last win coming in 2003 when Mauresmo and Pierce dominated the Americans in the final.

Volley

▲ Roger Federer about to return with a volley.

idea was to hit a hard, accurate service that forced the opponent into a lofted return that could be put away quickly by the incoming volleyer.

The slower the court, the harder it is to serve and volley. The reason for this is that a slower hard or clay court, providing a high, uniform bounce, allows the receiver more time to hit their return and potentially pass the server as they rush into the net.

Serve and volley exponents who enjoyed considerable success, particularly on fast surfaces such as the grass at Wimbledon, included Rod Laver, John McEnroe, Boris Becker, Martina Navratilova, Stefan Edberg, Pete Sampras and Goran Ivanisevic – but even Wimbledon sees less volleying nowadays. Some believe this is because the surface at the All England is slower than it used to be while others think racket technology has made it easier for returners to cope with ferocious serving.

At all the Grand Slam events, however, you will see some of the best volleyers in the world playing in the doubles events. In doubles, the pairing that dominates the net usually wins the point and servers almost always follow their shots to the net.

In recent times a style of tennis known as "serve and volley" was popular but it appears to be becoming a dying art. The

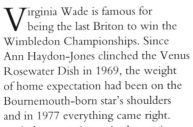

Wade

Virginia Wade is famous for being the last Briton to win the Wimbledon Championships. Since Ann Haydon-Jones clinched the Venus Rosewater Dish in 1969, the weight of home expectation had been on the Bournemouth-born star's shoulders and in 1977 everything came right.

A three-set victory in the semi-finals over defending champion Chris Evert set up a showdown with Betty Stove of the Netherlands, who had put out another Brit, 21-year-old Sue Barker. Wade lost the first set but rallied magnificently to win 4-6, 6-3, 6-1 in front of an ecstatic Centre Court crowd. What made the achievement even more noteworthy was that it came during the Queen's Silver Jubilee year and on the centenary of the very first championships.

What few people in the UK realise is that Wade was already 31 years old and a double Grand Slam title winner by the time she lifted the Wimbledon trophy. In 1968 she defeated the great Billie Jean King in the final of the US Open and four years later beat home favourite Evonne Goolagong to the Australian Open title.

◄ Virginia Wade lifts the trophy high above her head after beating Betty Stove in the Wimbledon ladies' final.

▼ Virginia Wade in action during the 1968 US Open.

Wheelchair Tennis

▶ Shingo Kunieda serving.

▼ Jiske Griffioen hits a return watched by her partner Esther Vergeer during the French Open final in 2008.

The rules of wheelchair tennis are principally the same as for able-bodied competitors with one exception: players are permitted to let the ball bounce twice.

The NEC Wheelchair Tennis Tour now encompasses more than 100 events with the Australian Open, Japanese Open, British Open and US Open holding Super Series – the equivalent of Grand Slam – status. The undisputed number one in the men's game is Shingo Kunieda. With eight titles to his name, including the men's singles at the Beijing Paralympic Games and three Grand Slam victories, the

25-year-old Japanese star was unbeaten at singles in 2008. What's more, he was ranked second at doubles behind compatriot Satoshi Saida.

In the women's game the Dutch dominated in 2008 with Esther Vergeer, Korie Homan and Jiske Griffioen holding the top three spots in the world rankings at the end of November. Also unbeaten at that stage of the year, Vergeer won the Paralympic women's singles gold medal (the third of her career) as well as the prestigious NEC Wheelchair Tennis Masters, where she defeated Britain's Lucy Shuker in the final. The Dutch star had held the number one spot since 1999.

Wheelchair tennis players can compete with or against able-bodied players, they alone observing the double-bounce rule.

Williams: Serena

She only played 13 tournaments in 2008 and still finished the year at number two in the rankings. Such is the awesome talent of Michigan-born star Serena Williams that she reached at least the quarter-finals of all but three of those events and won four of them. The fact of the matter is, regardless of her world ranking at the time, Williams is always one of the players to beat.

Able to deliver 120mph+ serves and producing breathtaking power from the back of the court, Serena displays great agility and a perhaps unmatched fighting spirit. These qualities have carried her to 10 Grand Slam singles victories and a total of 33 titles on the WTA Tour.

Having turned pro at 14, Williams was just 17 when she grabbed her first Big Four victory, at Flushing Meadows in 1999. There she defeated another teenage prodigy in the form of Switzerland's Martina Hingis 6-3, 7-6. But 2002 is the year that defines Serena's career to date. Having missed the Australian Open due to injury, she reeled off three successive Grand Slam singles finals wins against big sister

◀ Serena Williams got the better of sister Venus at the 2002 US Open.

▼ Serena Williams on her way to her first major success, Flushing Meadows, 1999.

Venus, grabbing the world number one spot during the process. Serena completed her "Career Grand Slam" at Melbourne the following year, again beating Venus in the final.

Williams: Venus

▲ Venus
Williams serves
against sister
Serena at
Wimbledon in
2008.

▶ Success in
Doha, 2008.

Had it not been for her equally gifted younger sister, who has beaten her in five finals, Venus Williams would surely have racked up even more than the seven Grand Slams she has on her CV.

While Serena may be edging her in terms of the Big Four, Venus has one title that still eludes her sibling – an Olympic singles gold medal. Having defeated fellow-American Monica Seles in a three-set semi-final at the Sydney Games of 2000, Venus triumphed 6-2, 6-4 over Elena Dementieva of Russia. She added a further gold in the doubles with her sister that year and the pair increased their Olympic haul in Beijing in 2008, defeating Spain's Anabel Medina Garrigues and Virginia Ruano Pascual in the final.

But it is on the grass courts of Wimbledon that Venus will forever be remembered. Displaying grace and athleticism as well as impressive power, the older Williams sister already has five All England ladies' singles titles to her name and, at 28 years old, has plenty of time to add to that tally.

A former world number one with more than $21 million banked in prize money, Williams closed 2008 in dominant fashion, winning the prestigious Sony Ericsson Championships.

Wimbledon

Once a year, the All England Club in Church Road, Wimbledon, hosts The Lawn Tennis Championship Meeting, one of the most famous events in world sport.

When, in 1877, Spencer Gore defeated William Marshall in the first Wimbledon men's singles final, he would have been unaware of the historical importance of his victory. Lawn tennis was a fledgling sport and just 22 players entered the tournament, Gore winning his final in front of a crowd of 200.

Today's tournament is unrecognisable from its humble beginnings. There are 128 players in both the men's and women's singles draws and many more take part in the qualifying tournaments at the Bank of England Sports Club in Roehampton. In addition more than 400,000 people visit the event each year and 15,000 are able to watch the singles finals on Centre Court.

Yet despite the fact it has moved with the times, tradition plays a very strong part at Wimbledon and no visit

◄ Prince Albert competing at Wimbledon in 1926.

to the All England would be complete without eating a bowl of strawberries and cream. In fact, so popular is the custom that an incredible 28,000kg of strawberries are consumed at Wimbledon each year, accompanied by 7,000l of fresh cream.

Unfortunately there is another, far less pleasant ritual in SW19 – diving for cover from the rain. The unpredictable

▲ Sir Cliff Richard orchestrates the singing as the crowd join in on another rain delayed day at Wimbledon.

▶ Rain frequently stops play at Wimbledon.

British weather has threatened to spoil many a Wimbledon Championships but the organisers invariably manage to see all the events through to a successful conclusion. Who can forget Sir Cliff Richard entertaining a frustrated crowd during yet another rain delay in 1996 or the deluges of 2001 that held back the men's singles final between Goran Ivanisevic and Patrick Rafter to an unprecedented third Monday?

The Croat's triumph that year marked the end of a 14-year journey but some players have enjoyed multiple successes at the championships. American great Pete Sampras shares the honour of having won seven men's singles titles with Britain's

William Renshaw, and in 1990 Martina Navratilova broke Helen Wills Moody's record with her ninth ladies' championship victory.

Navratilova, in fact, shares with Billie Jean King the record for overall highest number of titles at the All England, courtesy of nine singles, seven ladies' doubles and four mixed doubles victories. But Billie Jean wasn't the only King to appear at Wimbledon – in 1926, Prince Albert (who later became George VI) played in the men's doubles, losing in the first round.

Woodies

They won 11 Grand Slam men's titles together, Olympic gold medals and a record 61 doubles events in total – they even had the perfect names for a pairs team. Todd Woodbridge and Mark Woodforde of Australia – otherwise known as the "Woodies" – were a phenomenon in the game of tennis that brought much needed attention to an oft-overlooked discipline.

Strong singles players – each broke into the top 20 in the world and made Grand Slam singles semi-finals – when they played as a pairing there was an air of invincibility about them.

The proud possessors of five doubles titles at the All England, two Australian and two US Open Championships,

the French Open continued to elude them until 2000, the year of Woodforde's retirement. The pairing finally completed their career Grand Slam with victory on the red clay over Paul Haarhuis and Sandon Stolle and it was fitting that the win also broke the 57-title record held jointly by Peter Fleming/John McEnroe and Bob Hewitt/Frew McMillan. Signing off in style, the Woodies then claimed a final Wimbledon a month later.

Woodbridge went on to further Grand Slam glory partnering Sweden's Jonas Bjorkman and in 2004 became the most successful men's doubles player of all time at Wimbledon, courtesy of an eighth victory.

◀ Mark Woodforde and Todd Woodbridge hold the trophy aloft after victory in the men's doubles at the Australian Open.

▼ The Woodies had an air of invincibility about them.

X-Rated

Away from the genteel garden party image there is a racier side to the game of tennis.

Ever since Suzanne Lenglen dared to show a bit of leg in the 1920s and "Gorgeous" Gussie Moran opted for a short skirt and lace-trimmed frilly knickers at Wimbledon in 1949, sex and tennis have been inextricably linked.

One of the most famous poster images of the 1970s was of the "Tennis Girl", a photograph taken by Martin Elliot of a woman walking away from the camera while lifting her tennis dress to scratch a naked bottom. More than two million copies of the iconic image were sold and stars such as Anna Kournikova and Kylie Minogue have since paid photographic tributes to it.

While women's tennis has become increasingly glamorous and outfits more revealing, the men have also grabbed headlines for baring a bit of flesh, with the likes of Andre Agassi drawing gasps from the crowds at Wimbledon when changing shirts between games and Roger Federer recently appearing in a *People* magazine "International Men of Sexiness" feature.

You Cannot Be Serious!

Tennis players can be an amusing, angry, emotional and even insightful bunch and the game's history is full of interesting quotes.

Perhaps the simplest – and most famous – is John McEnroe's verbal volley of "You cannot be serious!" aimed at Wimbledon umpire Edward James in 1981. When James refused to rule a particular service "in" during McEnroe's match with Tom Gullikson, Supermac exploded with frustration, claiming "chalk flew up", and calling officials "the pits of the world".

But although they often vent their spleens at unfortunate officials it's important to remember that tennis players have a sense of humour. Take Vitas Gerulaitis' straight-faced words

to journalists at a press conference after he'd finally ended a 16-match losing streak against Jimmy Connors: "Nobody beats Vitas Gerulaitis 17 times in a row."

Venus Williams once gave a powerful insight into what makes a true champion. The five-time Wimbledon champion said: "In my mind, I'm always the best. If I walk out on court, and I think the other person is better, I've already lost."

But last word must go to the legendary Musketeer, Jean Borotra, who died in 1994 at the age of 95, and who sums up the tennis enthusiast's love for the game: "The only possible regret I have is the feeling that I will die without having played enough tennis."

▲ McEnroe frequently argued with the umpire.

◀ Gertrude "Gussie" Moran caused a furore with her outfits.

◀◀ Anna Kournikova's good looks drew plenty of admirers.

Youth

▲ Martina Hingis was one of the most successful young players of recent years.

▲▲ Victory came at a young age for Tracy Austin.

Numerous players have made an impact on the professional senior game at a surprisingly young age and you have to go right back to 1887 to find the youngest ever Grand Slam singles champion, Lottie Dod, who claimed Wimbledon aged just 15 years 285 days.

In the modern era, Martina Hingis set a host of records – in 1996, at 15 years nine months, she became the youngest Wimbledon ladies' doubles champion, and the following year was crowned youngest world number one and most youthful Grand Slam winner of the 20th century courtesy of victory at the Australian Open. In fact the women rule the roost when it comes to age-related Grand Slam victories, Tracy Austin and Monica Seles clinching the US Open and French titles respectively at 16.

In the men's game America's Michael Chang ended Mats Wilander's claim to being the youngest champion on the French clay, when, as a 17-year-old he defeated a positively ancient, 23-year-old Stefan Edberg. Boris Becker won Wimbledon in 1985 at the same age and Pete Sampras had just turned 19 when he picked up the US Open of 1990. Australia's Ken Rosewall was the youngest men's winner of his home Grand Slam, claiming the title aged 18 in 1953.

Zen

To compete at a high level you need to be fit, strong and technically faultless. But perhaps the most important factor in the upper echelons of the game is mental toughness.

The most famous master of the inner game was Bjorn Borg. Known as "Iceborg" due to his on-court persona where he appeared to be in complete control of his emotions, he employed a methodical approach to life on tour – staying at the same hotels and eating at the same restaurants. The Swede was the epitome of inner calm but this wasn't always the case – as a junior, Borg was temperamental and argumentative on court, so much so that he was even banned from his local club for five months.

Another Swede who always appeared at ease on the court was double Wimbledon champion Stefan Edberg, who used to hide his head under a towel during end changes in an apparent state of meditation.

In the women's game Chris Evert – known as the "Ice Maiden" in her early career due to her unflustered demeanour during matches and baseline consistency – Martina Navratilova and Monica Seles stand out as figures of mental strength.

▼ Borg was renowned for his cool temperament.

Zoom!

In the right hands a powerful serve is the most destructive weapon in tennis and many top players have built their games around it.

Goran Ivanisevic served an incredible 212 aces at Wimbledon the year he won the championship, and recorded speeds in excess of 130mph during his career. But the Croatian does not possess the fastest service in the history of men's tennis. That honour goes to America's Andy Roddick with his unstoppable 155mph effort (249.4kph) in the 2004 Davis Cup. Roddick uses his service to excellent effect on the men's ATP Tour – not only did he win 91% of his service games during 2008 (more than any other player), he took 80% of his first-service points and bagged 889 aces in 62 matches,

the latter figure bettered only by 6ft 10in Ivo Karlovic of Croatia.

It's not just the top men who can serve bullets – Venus Williams hit a 129mph effort in the French Open of 2007 and Brenda Schultz-McCarthy of the Netherlands reached the 130mph mark during qualifying in Cincinnati in 2006. The women's WTA Tour also produces a "Power Index" which shows players' average maximum hitting speeds, taking serves, groundstrokes, returns and smashes into consideration. Over the course of four events in 2008 America's Lindsay Davenport was the hardest hitter while Maria Sharapova of Russia was fourth.

The pictures in this book were provided courtesy of the following:

GETTY IMAGES
101 Bayham Street, London NW1 0AG

Creative Director: Kevin Gardner

Design and Artwork: David Wildish

Picture research: Ellie Charleston

Published by Green Umbrella Publishing

Publishers Jules Gammond and Vanessa Gardner

Written by John Thynne